WAR, The
And AN

VLADIMIR SOLOVIEV

WAR, THE CHRISTIAN, And ANTI-CHRIST

Including

THE THREE DISCUSSIONS

Соловьев Владимир Сергеевич

New Edition
by
William G. von Peters, Ph.D.

Catholic Resources
Chattanooga
MCMXIII

Copyright © 2013, Dr. William G. von Peters. All U.S., International and World rights reserved in all media formats. No part of this book may be reproduced in any form, or by any means, without permission from the Dr. William G. von Peters.

CONTENTS

		PAGE
	PREFACE	i
	FOREWORD	v
	INTRODUCTION	1
	THE BACKDROP	9
I.	The First Discussion	11
II.	The Second Discussion	39
III.	The Third Discussion	75
IV.	A Brief Novella About Anti-Christ	109

APPENDIX

The Anti-Christ Unmasked	139
Vladimir Soloviev on God Using Unbelievers	165
Vladimir Sergeyevich Soloviev on the Antichrist	166

PREFACE

VLADIMIR SOLOVIEV, the author of the book, is a lost treasure. He was a perfected soul, Russia's greatest philosopher, one of her greatest poets, and a prophet for the reunion of the Russian Orthodox Church with the Catholic Church — which he preferred to call the "Universal Church."

At the end of the 19th Century Soloviev was well known in Russia and abroad. His name was on par with that of Dostoyevsky and Tolstoy, a bright shining light of truth. But with the rise of Bolshevism, Lenin had his works suppressed, and so knowledge of him was gradually lost to the Soviet Bloc and in the West.

With the fall of Communism, Soloviev has been resurrected within Russia as a great thinker, and slowly his name is becoming better known in the West as more discover him. A fervent Christian, Soloviev believed that the Faith is not lived in the church on Sunday, but must permeate and guide society. In a word, society must be converted to Christ.

Soloviev is the author of the opus "Russia and the Universal Church"[1], wherein he shows that there is and can be only one "one holy Catholic and apostolic Church" of Jesus Christ, under the rule of he whom Christ appointed and his successors – the Popes; and that the Orthodox, as long as they remain separated, will be stagnant and incomplete in the Faith.

Soloviev lived and died as a Russian Orthodox, who came to personal union with the Universal (Catholic) Church. He was an ascetic, of the Franciscan type, living his life in pursuit of the Wisdom of God. This concept of the Wisdom of God (now all but forgotten, but enshrined in the Hagia Sophia of Constantinople) is identified with our Lady, and she appeared to him three times, guiding his path as he worked out his understanding of God, the Church, the papacy and his salvation.

This work, comprising the Three Discussions, has been previously published under several names. The third discussion, the "Brief Novella About Anti–Christ"[2], has been published separately under various names as well.

I have chosen to title this edition, War, the Christian, and Anti–Christ, as these are the subjects of Soloviev's efforts.

In our age the question of whether Christians can support war is becoming more and more pertinent to Americans as the American Empire

---

[1] Available at the www.lulu.com/rheims website.
[2] The literal translation of Soloviev's Russian title for this section. A novella being a short novel or story, especially one which teaches a moral message.

wages war throughout the world. Many hold that Christ would have us be pacifists, and not lift our hands against another man; even if he were to kill us. Others believe that the innate goodness in man is trainable to overcome war and abolish it through 'love'.

Soloviev traces these ideas to Count Leo Tolstoy, who taught a social gospel which sounds remarkably modern and "New Age" as Soloviev gives its arguments and responds with a Christian understanding that we greatly need in the 21st Century.

And then there is Anti–Christ. A prophet, as well as a philosopher, Soloviev gives us information about the rise of the political and economic system that allows Anti–Christ to first gain control of Europe, and then the world. He presciently predicts the modern political correctness of our age, the rise of China and the East, the European Union and more; and most importantly he instructs us in the difference between true good and false good.

Then he reveals to us the reunion of the various churches with the Catholic Church in the face of the force of Anti–Christ's false church and persecution of true Christians; leading to Christ's return. So Soloviev ends this, his last work, completed only three months before his death, with a message of hope for us.

I have taken several translations of his work and blended them to get the best, most readable translation for modern readers. A foreword has been added consisting of an article by Cardinal Biffi on Soloviev and Anti–Christ. An appendix has been added containing an article by Abbé Georges de Nantes entitled "Unmasking the Anti–Christ" which gives further understanding to this work; Soloviev's short admonition on God using unbelievers to accomplish his work, and a newer talk by Cardinal Biffi on Soloviev and the Anti-Christ.

St. John of the Cleft Rock (14th century) said: "It is said that twenty centuries after the Incarnation of the Word, the Beast in its turn shall become man. About the year 2000 A.D., Antichrist will reveal himself to the world."

Is it possible that we are indeed living in the years preparatory to the rise of Anti-Christ?

St. John was not the only saint to prophesy about our time. St. Nilus in 430 A.D. said:

> After the year 1900, toward the middle of the 20th century, the people of that time will become unrecognizable. When the time for the Advent of the Antichrist approaches, people's

minds will grow cloudy from carnal passions, and dishonor and lawlessness will grow stronger. Then the world will become unrecognizable.

People's appearances will change, and it will be impossible to distinguish men from women due to their shamelessness in dress and style of hair. These people will be cruel and will be like wild animals because of the temptations of the Antichrist. There will be no respect for parents or elders, love will disappear, and Christian pastors, bishops, and priests will become vain men, completely failing to distinguish the right hand way from the left.

At that time the morals and traditions of Christians and the Church will change. People will abandon modesty, and dissipation will reign. Falsehood and greed will attain great proportions, and woe to those who pile up treasures. Lust, adultery, homosexuality, secret deeds and murder will rule in society.

It certainly sounds like he was commenting on the latest news stories in America concerning political correctness and disappearing morality.

St. Cyril of Jerusalem wrote in 386 AD that "Antichrist will exceed in malice, perversity, lust, wickedness, impiety, ruthlessness and barbarity all men that have ever disgraced human nature..." Thus we have an idea of the Anti-Christ as someone mean, ugly and brutal — a Stalin for example. But while Anti-Christ will be all of these things in secret, Soloviev tells us that this man will be cloaked in light as a man of brilliance, a pacifist, ecologist and ecumenist. A New Age man, who is a vegetarian, a fighter for animal rights. A man people will want to follow because of his sheer brilliance.

Thus war, pacifism, the Christian and Anti-Christ intertwined are Soloviev's message that he left us as he prepared to depart this life at the young age of 47, worn out in the work of God.

It is quite possible that Soloviev is *the* prophet for our age. A voice giving both warning, and hope. A saint as yet unproclaimed, he speaks yet to us.

Dr. William G. von Peters, Ph.D.
Advent, Year of our Lord 2013

"True spiritual love is not a feeble imitation and anticipation of death, but a triumph over death, not a separation of the immortal form from the mortal, of the eternal from the temporal, but a transfiguration of the mortal into the immortal, the acceptance of the temporal into the eternal. False spirituality is a denial of the flesh; true spirituality is the regeneration of the flesh, its salvation, its resurrection from the dead."

— Vladimir Soloviev, *The Meaning of Love*

FOREWORD

Antichrist Alert! Cardinal Biffi Rouses the Church

The archbishop emeritus of Bologna delves back into the famous story by Vladimir Soloviev and applies it to the Christianity of today.

by Sandro Magister

ROMA, June 3, 2005 – Cardinal Giacomo Biffi, now 77, was archbishop of Bologna from 1984 to 2003. A theologian and a great scholar of Saint Ambrose, he has assembled some of his writings which are not strictly theological in a volume recently published by Cantagalli.

The title of the book: "Pinocchio, Peppone, l'Anticristo e altre divagazioni [Pinocchio, Peppone, the Antichrist, and other Meanderings]."

The Antichrist referred to in the title is the one described by Russian philosopher and theologian Vladimir Sergeyevich Soloviev in the last book he wrote before his death in 1900: "The Three Dialogues and the Story of the Antichrist."

Why does Cardinal Biffi want to bring this back to everyone's attention today? Because – he writes – "Soloviev announces with prophetic clarity the great crisis that afflicted Christianity during the last decade of the 20th century."

In the figure of the Antichrist as described by Soloviev, Biffi sees "the emblem of the confused and ambiguous religious identity of the times we are living in now." He sees the singling out and criticism of "principled Christianity," an emphasis on "openness," obsession with "dialogue" at all costs, "in which there seems to remain little of the unique and incomparable person of the Son of God who was crucified for us, rose from the dead, and is now alive. It is the situation that Fr. Divo Barsotti denounced in an extraordinary, and extraordinarily true, statement, when he said that in the Catholic world of our time, Jesus Christ is too often simply an excuse to talk about something else."

In Soloviev's tale, the Antichrist is elected president of the United States of Europe, acclaimed as emperor in Rome, takes possession of the entire world, and finally imposes his command even over the life and organization of the Churches. But what Cardinal Biffi calls to attention is not this series of events, but rather the personal characteristics of the Antichrist. Here follow a few passages from his essay, which deserves to be read in its entirety, in which the cardinal summarizes these personal traits and explains what lesson they hold for the Church of today:

The days are coming, and are already here...

by Giacomo Biffi

The Antichrist, says Soloviev, was "a convinced spiritualist." He believed in goodness, and even in God. He was an ascetic, a scholar, a philanthropist. He gave "the greatest possible demonstrations of moderation, disinterest, and active beneficence."

In his early youth, he had distinguished himself as a talented and insightful exegete: one of his extensive works on biblical criticism had brought him an honorary degree from the University of Tübingen.

But the book that had gained for him universal fame and consensus bore the title: "The Open Road to Universal Peace and Prosperity," in which "a noble respect for ancient traditions and symbols was joined with a sweeping, audacious radicalism toward social and political needs and directives. Limitless freedom of thought was united with a profound comprehension of everything mystical; absolute individualism with an ardent dedication to the common good; the most elevated idealism toward guiding principles with the complete precision and viability of practical solutions."

It is true that some men of faith wondered why the name of Christ did not appear even once, but others replied: "If the contents of the book are permeated with the true Christian spirit, with active love and universal benevolence, what more do you want?" Besides, he "was not in principle hostile to Christ." On the contrary, he appreciated his right intentions and lofty teaching.

But three things about Jesus were unacceptable to him.

First of all, his moral preoccupations. "The Christ," he asserted, "has divided men according to good and evil with his moralism, whereas I will unite them with the benefits that both good and evil alike require."

He also did not like Christ's "absolute uniqueness." He was one of many, or even better – he said – he was my precursor, because I am the perfect and definitive savior; I have purified his message of what is unacceptable for the men of today.

Finally, and above all, he could not endure the fact that Christ is alive, so much so that he repeated hysterically: "He is not among the living, and will never be. He is not risen, he is not risen, he is not risen. He rotted, he rotted in the tomb..."

But where Soloviev's presentation shows itself to be particularly original and surprising – and merits greater reflection – is in the attribution to the Antichrist of the qualities of pacifist, environmentalist, ecumenist. [...]

Did Soloviev have a particular person in mind when he made this description of the Antichrist? It is undeniable that he alludes above all to the "new Christianity" that Leo Tolstoy was successfully promoting during those years. [...]

In his "Gospel," Tolstoy reduces all of Christianity to five rules of conduct which he derives from the Sermon on the Mount:

1. Not only must you not kill, but you must not even become angry with your brother.

2. You must not give in to sensuality, not even to the desire for your own wife.

3. You must never bind yourself by swearing an oath.

4. You must not resist evil, but you must apply the principle of non–violence to the utmost and in every case.

5. Love, help, and serve your enemy.

According to Tolstoy, although these precepts come from Christ, they in no way require the actual existence of the Son of the living God to be valid. [...]

Of course, Soloviev does not specifically identify the great novelist with the figure of the Antichrist. But he intuited with extraordinary clairvoyance that Tolstoy's creed would become during the 20th century the vehicle of the substantial nullification of the gospel message, under the formal exaltation of an ethics and a love for humanity presented as Christian "values." [...]

The days will come, Soloviev tells us – and are already here, we say – in which the salvific meaning of Christianity, which can be received only in a difficult, courageous, concrete, and rational act of faith, will be dissolved into a series of "values" easily sold on the world markets.

The greatest of the Russian philosophers warns us that we must guard against this danger. Even if a Tolstoian Christianity were to make us infinitely more acceptable in the living room, at social and political gatherings, and on television, we cannot and must not renounce the Christianity of Jesus Christ, the Christianity that has at its center the scandal of the cross and the astonishing reality of the Lord's resurrection.

Jesus Christ, the crucified and risen Son of God, the only savior of mankind, cannot be transformed into a series of worthwhile projects and good inspirations, which are part and parcel of the dominant worldly mentality. Jesus Christ is a "rock," as he said of himself. And one either builds upon this "rock" (by entrusting oneself) or lunges against it (through opposition): "He who falls on this stone will be broken to pieces; but when it falls on any one, it will crush him" (Mt. 21:44). [...]

So Soloviev's teaching was simultaneously prophetic and largely ignored. But we want to repropose it in the hope that Christianity will finally catch on to it and pay it a bit of attention.

The new book by Giacomo Cardinal Biffi from which the passage on the Antichrist was taken:

Giacomo Biffi, "Pinocchio, Peppone, l'Anticristo e altre divagazioni [Pinocchio, Peppone, the Antichrist, and other Meanderings]," Cantagalli, Siena, 2005, pp. 256.

The Antichrist is referred to in three passages of the New Testament.

The first letter of John, 4:3 : "Every spirit which does not confess Jesus is not of God. This is the spirit of Antichrist, of which you heard that it was coming, and now it is in the world already."

The second letter of John, 1:7 : "For many deceivers have gone out into the world, men who will not acknowledge the coming of Jesus Christ in the flesh; such a one is a deceiver and the Antichrist."

The second letter of Paul to the Thessalonians, 2:3–5 : "Let no one deceive you in any way; for that day will not come, unless the rebellion comes first, and the man of lawless is revealed, the son of perdition, who opposes and exalts himself against every so-called God or object of worship, so that he takes his seat in the temple of God, proclaiming himself to be God. Do you not remember that when I was still with you I told you this?"

3.6.2005

http://chiesa.espresso.repubblica.it/articolo/32418?eng=y

INTRODUCTION

Is evil only a natural defect, an imperfection disappearing of itself with the growth of good, or is it a real *power,* possessing our world by means of temptations, so that for fighting it successfully assistance must be found in another sphere of being? This vital question can be fully examined and solved only in a complete system of metaphysics.

I began carrying out this task for those who are capable of contemplation,[3] but I soon felt how important the problem of evil is for everybody. Some two years ago a change in the tenor of my spiritual life, which there is no need to dwell upon just now, created in me a strong and firm desire to illumine in some clear and easy way the main aspects of the problem of evil, which must concern everybody.

For a long time I was unable to find a suitable medium for carrying out my plan. In the spring of 1899, however, during my stay abroad, I spontaneously composed and wrote in a few days the First Discussion on this subject, and on returning to Russia wrote the two others. In this way I discovered the literary form which this work assumes, and which provided me with the simplest medium for the expression of the thoughts I was desirous of communicating.

This form of drawing–room discussion is a sufficient proof in itself that neither a scientifico–philosophical examination nor an orthodox sermon should be looked for in this work. My object in it was rather apologetic and polemic: I endeavored, as far as I could, to set out clearly and prominently the vital aspects of Christian truth, in so far as it is connected with the question of evil, and to disperse the fog with which everybody seems to have been trying lately to enwrap it.

Many years ago I happened to read about a new religion that was founded in the eastern provinces of Russia. The religion, the followers of which called themselves "Hole–drillers," or "Hole–worshippers," was very simple; a middle–sized hole was drilled in a wall in some dark corner of a house, and the men put their mouths to it and repeated earnestly: "My house, my hole, do save me!"

Never before, I believe, has the object of worship been reduced to such a degree of simplicity. It must be admitted, however, that though the worship of an ordinary peasant's house, and of a simple hole made by human hands in its wall, was a palpable error, it was a truthful error; those men were absolutely mad, but they did not deceive anybody; the

---

[3] The introduction to this work was published by me in the first three chapters of my "Theoretical Philosophy."

house they worshipped they called a *house,* and the hole drilled in the wall they reasonably termed merely *a hole.*

But the religion of the hole-worshippers soon underwent a process of "evolution," and was subjected to "transformation." It still retained in its new form its former weakness of religious thought and its narrow character of philosophic interests, its former *terre-a-terre* realism, but it completely lost its past truthfulness.

The "house" now was termed "the Kingdom of God on Earth," and the "hole" received the name of "the new Gospel," whilst the distinction between the sham gospel and the true one (and this is the most distressing fact about it), a distinction which is exactly similar to that existing between a hole drilled in a beam, and complete living tree—this essential distinction was either neglected or confused by the new evangelists.

Of course, I do not assert a direct historical or "genetic" connection between the original sect of hole-worshippers and the teaching of the sham Kingdom of God and the sham Gospel. Neither is it important for my object, which is only to show clearly the essential identity of the two "teachings" with that moral distinction which has been stated above. The identity here lies in the purely negative and void character of both "doctrines."

It is true, the "educated" hole-worshippers do not call themselves by this name, but go under the name of Christians, and their teaching is also passed as the Gospel, but Christianity without Christ, and the Gospel, *i.e.,* the *"message of good,"* without the only good worth announcing, *viz.,* without the real resurrection to the fullness of blessed life—these are as much a hollow space as is the ordinary hole drilled in a peasant's house.

There would not be any need to speak about this at all were it not for the fact that over the rationalist hole the Christian flag is flown, tempting and confusing many of the "little ones." When the people who believe and cautiously declare that Christ has become *obsolete* and has been *superseded,* or that He never existed at all, and that His life is a myth invented by Paul, at the same time persistently call themselves "true Christians" and screen their teaching of hollow space by distorted quotations from the Gospel, it is well-nigh time to put aside our indifference to, and our condescending contempt for, their opinions.

The moral atmosphere is contaminated with systematic falsehoods, so the public conscience loudly demands that the evil work should be branded by its real name. The true object of polemics would in this case be *not the confuting of sham religion but the showing up of the actual fraud.*

This fraud has no excuse. Between me, as the author of three books, banned by the ecclesiastic censorship on the one side, and these publishers of numerous foreign books, pamphlets, and leaflets on the other side, the question of external obstacles for an unreserved frankness in these matters does not seriously arise.

The restraints of religious freedom, existing in our country, cause the greatest pain to my heart, for I see and feel to what a great extent these external restrictions bring harm to and impose burdens not only on those whom they directly hit, but mainly on the cause of Christianity in Russia, consequently on the Russian nation, consequently, again, on the Russian State.

No external situation can prevent a man who is honestly convinced in his opinions, stating them fully. If it is impossible to do so at home, one can do it abroad, and no one has availed himself of this opportunity to a greater extent than the teachers of the sham Gospel have done when the matters concerned have been the *practical* questions of politics and religion.

Whilst as regards the main, the essential question there is no need even to go abroad in order to refrain from insincerity and artifice: the Russian censorship never demands that anybody should pronounce opinions that he does not hold, to simulate a faith in things he does not believe in, or to love and revere what he despises and hates. To maintain an honest attitude towards the known historical Person and His Work, the preachers of hollowness had only one thing to do in Russia: they should merely have "ignored" Him.

But here is the strange fact: in this matter these men refuse to avail themselves either of the freedom of silence which they enjoy at home or of the freedom of speech which they enjoy abroad. Both here and there they prefer to show their allegiance to the Gospel of Christ; both here and there they decline to reveal honestly their real attitude to the Founder of Christianity either by a resolute word or by an eloquent silence, *i.e.,* to show that He is entirely alien to them, is for no object required and is only a hindrance in their way.

From their point of view the things they preach are *of themselves* clear, desirable and salutary for everybody. Their "truth" is self-supporting, and if a certain historical person happens to agree with it, so much is it the better for him, though this fact does not endow him with any special authority in their eyes, particularly when it is remembered that this person had said and done many things which for these people are nothing but a "temptation" and "madness."

Even supposing that these moralists in their very human weakness feel an irresistible desire to sustain their beliefs as well as their own "reason" by some historical authority, why, I ask, do they not look in history for *another* who shall be a more suitable representative?

There has for a long time been one waiting for such recognition—the founder of the widely–popular religion of Buddhism. He did really preach what they required: non–resistance, impossibility, inactivity, sobriety, etc., and succeeded even *without a martyrdom* to "make a brilliant career" for his religion. The sacred books of the Buddhists do really proclaim *hollowness,* and to make them fully agree with the new teaching of the same matter they would require only a little simplification in detail.

On the contrary, the Scriptures of the Jews and Christians are filled and permeated throughout by a positive spiritual message which denies both ancient and modern emptiness, so that to be able to fasten the teaching of this latter to any of the statements taken from the Gospel or the Prophets it is necessary, by hook or by crook, to tear away such a statement from its natural connection with the whole of the book and the context. Whereas, on the other hand, the Buddhist "suttee" supplies whole masses of suitable parables and legends, and there is nothing in those books inimical in spirit to the new teaching.

By substituting the hermit of the Shakyas tribe for the "rabbi from Galilee," the sham Christians would have lost nothing of importance, but would win something very valuable indeed, at least in my eyes —they would win the possibility of being, even while erring, honestly thinking and to an extent consistent. But they do not want this. . . .

The hollowness of the teaching of the new religion and its logical contradictions are too apparent, and in this matter I have been satisfied to give (in the Third Discussion) only a brief, though complete, statement of their pronouncements, obviously contradictory in themselves and hardly capable of tempting anybody outside the hopeless class of people typified by my Prince. Should I succeed in opening anybody's eyes to the other side of the question and making any deceived but living soul feel all the moral falsity of this death–spreading teaching taken in all its entirety, the polemical object of this book would be fully achieved.

I am firmly convinced, however, that the exposure of an untruth made without reservation, should it even fail to produce any beneficent effect, still remains, apart from the fulfillment of duty it involves for its author, a measure of spiritual sanitation in the life of society, and brings useful results both in the present and in the future.

Bound up with the polemical object of these dialogues I also pursue a positive aim: to present the question of the struggle against evil and of the meaning of history from three different standpoints. One of these is based on a religious conception of the everyday life, which is characteristic of past times, and is given much prominence in the First Discussion in the speeches of *the General.*

The other, representing the ideas of culture and progress as prevailing in our time, is expressed and defended by *the Politician,* particularly in the Second Discussion. Lastly, the third standpoint, which is absolutely religious and which will yet show its decisive value in the future, is indicated in the Third Discussion in the speeches of *Mr. Z.* and in the story by Father Pansophius.

Personally, I unreservedly accept the last point of view. But I fully recognize the relative truth contained in the two others, and for this reason could with equal fairness express the opposing arguments and statements of *the Politician* and *the General.* The higher absolute truth does not exclude or deny the preliminary conditions of its realization, but justifies, appreciates, and sanctifies them.

If from a certain point of view the world's history is God's judgment of the world—*die Weltgeschichte ist das Weltgericht*—this involves a long and complicated contest or litigation between the good and the evil historical forces, and this contest, to come to a final solution, must needs involve both a determined struggle for existence between those forces, and their greater inner, therefore peaceful, development in the common forms of culture.

For this reason the General and the Politician are both right in the light of the Higher truth, and I could with complete sincerity place myself in the position of the one or the other. It is only the power of evil itself that is absolutely wrong, but not such means of fighting it as the sword of the soldier or the pen of the diplomat. These *weapons* must be appraised at their actual usefulness in the given circumstances, and that must be considered the better of the two whose use is more effective in upholding the cause of good.

St. Alexis the metropolitan, when peacefully pleading for the Russian princes at the Tartar Horde, and St. Sergius when blessing the arms of Dmitrius of the Don against the same Horde—both equally served one and the same cause of good—that finds its expression in many various forms and fashions.

These discussions about evil and the militant and the peaceful methods of combating it, had to be concluded with a definite statement of the last, the most extreme manifestation of evil in history, the picture of its short–lived triumph and its final destruction.

At first I treated this subject in the form of a dialogue, as I had treated the other parts, and with a similar sprinkling of the jocular element. But friendly criticisms convinced me that this method of exposition was doubly unsuitable: firstly, because the interruptions and interpolations required by the form of dialogue tended to weaken the interest in the story; and, secondly, because the colloquial and particularly the jocular character of conversation did not accord with the religious importance of the subject.

I recognized the justice of these criticisms and accordingly altered the form of the Third Discussion, introducing in it the reading from a manuscript left by a monk after his death, of an independent "Brief Novella About Anti–Christ."[4] This story, which earlier formed the subject of a public lecture, created a good deal of bewilderment and confused comment on the platform and in the Press, the main reason for which appears to be very simple: the prevailing insufficient knowledge of the references to Anti–Christ contained in the Scriptures and in Church tradition.

These give indications of all the main features of Anti–Christ, such as the inner significance of Anti–Christ as a religious impostor, who obtains the title of the Son of God by "stealing" it, and not by spiritual self–sacrifice; his connection with a false prophet, wizard, who seduces people by means of real and false miracles; the obscure and peculiarly sinful origin of Anti–Christ himself, who secures his external position of a monarch of the world by the help of evil powers; lastly, the general development and the end of his activity.

Other particulars, characteristic of Anti–Christ and his false prophet, may also be found in the same sources. We have there, for instance, "bringing down fire from Heaven," murdering the two witnesses of Christ, exposure of their bodies in the streets of Jerusalem, and many others.

To connect the events with each other and to make the story more speaking several details had to be introduced, partly based on historical conjectures, and partly created by imagination. On the details of the latter kind, such as the semi–psychic, semi–conjuring tricks of the great magician with subterranean voices, fireworks, etc., I placed, it hardly needs saying, very little importance, and I think was justified in expecting a similar attitude on the part of my "critics." As regards the other and extremely essential point — the characteristics of the three impersonated confessions in the ecumenical council, this could be

---

[4] Краткая повесть об антихристе, Ed.

noticed and fully appreciated only by those of my critics who were acquainted with the history and life of the churches.

The character of the false prophet given in the Revelation and his mission, as clearly indicated therein, to mystify people for the benefit of Anti–Christ, made it necessary for me to attribute to him different prodigies of the kind that is peculiar to magicians and conjurers. It is known for certainty, *dass zein hauptwerk ein Feuerwerk sein wird :"* and he doeth great wonders, so that he maketh fire come down from heaven on the earth in the sight of men." (Apocalypse 13:13.)

At present we cannot, of course, know magic and mechanical technique of these prodigies, but we may be sure that in two or three centuries it will advance very far from what it is now, and what will be made possible by such progress for a magician like ours — is not for me to say. I have admitted to my story certain definite features and details only as concrete illustrations to the essential and fully–established relations, so that they would not be left mere bare schemes.

The essential and the details should also be clearly distinguished in all that I say about Pan–Mongolism and the Asiatic invasion of Europe. But, of course, the main fact itself has not in this case the absolute certainty which characterizes the future coming and the fate of Anti–Christ and his false prophet.

Nothing has been taken direct from the Scriptures in describing the development of the Mongolo–European relations, though a great deal of it can be based on Scriptural statements. Taken in general, the history indicated presents a series of conjectures of the probable based on the actual facts. Personally, I believe this probability to be very near the certainty, and this appears so, not only to me, but also to many much more important personages.

For the sake of coherency of the story, several details had to be introduced into these considerations of the coming Mongolian menace, for which I, of course, cannot vouch, and which, on the whole, were sparingly used. The thing of much greater importance to me was to make the picture of the coming terrific conflict of the two worlds as realistic as possible, and to show thereby the pressing necessity of peace and true friendship amongst all the nations of Europe.

If the general cessation of war seems to me impossible before the final catastrophe is over, I firmly believe that the closest friendship and peaceful cooperation of all the Christian nations and States is not only a possible but a necessary and morally imperative way for the salvation of the Christian world from being swallowed up by the lower elements.

So as not to make the story too long and too complicated I had to leave out another conjecture of mine which deserves a few words of explanation. It seems to me that the coming success of Pan–Mongolism will be greatly facilitated by the stubborn and exhaustive struggle which some of the European countries will have to wage against the awakened Islam in Western Asia and in the North and Central Africa.

A greater part than it is generally believed will be played in that awakening by the secret and incessant activity of the religious and political brotherhood of "Senussi," which has for the movements of modern Mohammedanism the same directing importance as in the movements of the Buddhistic world belongs to the Tibetan brotherhood of "Kelani," in Lhasa, with all its Indian, Chinese, and Japanese ramifications. I am far from being absolutely hostile to Buddhism, neither am I particularly so to Islam. But a willful blindness to the existing and coming state of things is too readily indulged in by many people today, and I might perhaps have chosen for myself a more profitable occupation.

The historical forces reigning over the masses of humanity will yet have to come to blows and become intermingled with each other before the new head grows on the self–lacerating body of the beast: the world–unifying power of the Anti–Christ, who "will speak high–sounding and splendid words," and will cast a glittering veil of good and truth over the mystery of utter lawlessness in the time of its final revelation, so that even the chosen, in the words of the Scriptures, will be reduced to the great betrayal. To show beforehand this deceptive visor was my highest aim in writing this book.

...I still feel numerous defects of the work. But not less felt is also the distant image of pale death, which quietly advises me not to put off the publication of this book to an indefinite and little secure date. Shall I be given time for new works, I shall be given it for improving the old ones as well. If not—the statement of the coming historical issue of the moral struggle has been made by me in sufficiently clear, though brief, outlines, and I publish this little work with the grateful feeling of a fulfilled moral duty.

VLADIMIR SOLOVIEV.

Easter, 1900.

This preface was originally published in the newspaper, *Rossiya*, under the title *"On the False Good."*

THE BACKDROP

IN the garden of one of those villas which, at the foot of the Alps, look down on the blue depths of the Mediterranean, there met one summer five Russians.

The first was an old GENERAL, a man of war from his youth, we shall call him the General. The second was a statesman, a politician, a "father of the Senate," resting from the whirl and turmoil of politics, we shall call him the POLITICIAN. The third was a young prince, a moralist and popular teacher, whose strong democratic views and thirst for reform had led him to publish a large number of various more or less helpful pamphlets on moral and social progress, we shall call him the PRINCE. The fourth was a middle-aged lady, very inquisitive and greatly interested in all that concerns human beings, she is the LADY; and the fifth was a gentleman of somewhat uncertain age and social position, let us call him MR. Z.

I was a silent listener to all their conversations, some of which appeared to me to have much interest, and whilst they were fresh in my memory I wrote them down. The first conversation was begun in my absence. I believe it started *apropos* of some newspaper article or peace pamphlet on the subject of the campaign against war and military service, a campaign originated by Count Tolstoy, which was being carried on by the Baroness Luttner and Mr. Stead, following in the footsteps of Tolstoy.

The POLITICIAN, on being asked by the LADY whether he thought the peace movement was a good one, gave it as his opinion that it was well-intentioned and useful. At that, the GENERAL got angry and began to make satirical jests at the expense of these three leaders of this anti-wa crusade, calling them the true pillars of State wisdom, guiding stars on the political horizon, even calling them the three "whales"[5] of Russia.

The POLITICIAN remarked, "Well there may be other *fish besides*." This remark caused MR. Z. to collapse with laughter, and he forced both the speakers to confess that they considered a whale was a fish, and even persuaded them to give a definition of what they thought a fish to be, that is, an animal belonging partly to the Admiralty and partly to the Department of Waterways.

I think, however, this was pure invention of MR. Z. Be that as it may, I was not fortunate enough to reconstruct the real beginning of the

---

[5] According to the Russian folklore the Earth rests on three whales.

conversation. Being afraid to compose out of my own head after the model of Plato and his imitators, I began my transcript with the words of the General which I heard as I approached the speakers.

WAR, THE CHRISTIAN, AND THE ANTI-CHRIST

FIRST DISCUSSION

" Audiatur et prima pars."

GENERAL *(agitated, stands up and then sits down again, speaking in rapid gestures).—* Oh, no! How is that? Oh, no! no! Answer me this one question: does a "Christ–serving and glorious Russian Army"[6] truly exist at this moment? Yes or no?

POLITICIAN *(lounging comfortably in an easy–chair, and speaking in a tone suggestive of a compound of Epicurus, a Prussian colonel, and Voltaire).—*Does a Russian Army exist? Obviously it exists. Surely you haven't heard that it had been abolished?

GENERAL.—Now, don't be ingenuous. You understand perfectly well that that is not what I mean. I ask you this: Am I right in regarding our present Army as a glorious band of Christ–loving warriors, or am I to suppose that one should call it something else?

POLITICIAN.— I see! That is what bothers you, is it? Well, you have brought your question to the wrong shop. You should inquire at the Department of Heraldry—they are the recognized experts in titles, I believe.

MR. Z.— *(speaking as if he had an idea at the back of his mind).* The Department of Heraldry will probably tell the General that the law places no restriction on the use of old titles. Did not the last Prince Lusignan hold the title of King of Cyprus, although he not only had no jurisdiction in Cyprus, but could not even drink Cyprian wine owing to his weak stomach and empty purse. So why shouldn't our contemporary army have the title of a Christ–loving band of warriors?

GENERAL.—Entitled? Is white or black a title? Is sweet or bitter a title? Hero or scoundrel—are they titles?

MR. Z.—Yes, of course. I wasn't giving my own point of view, but rather that which appears to be held by people who should know!

LADY *(to the Politician).* — Why do you argue about mere forms of expression? I am sure the General has more to say about his "Christ–loving band of warriors."

---

[6] A traditional title of the Russian army.

GENERAL.—Thank you, madam. What I wished, and what I still wish to say is this: From the earliest times until but yesterday every warrior, be he private or field-marshal, knew and felt that he served in a good and holy cause. He believed not only that he fulfilled duties every bit as necessary as sanitation or washing, for instance, but that he was part of . a service which was good, honorable, and noble in the highest sense of the word, and to which the greatest and best men that have ever lived—heroes and leaders of nations—have given their lives. This cause of ours has always been sanctified and exalted by the Church, and glorified by the praise of the nation.

Yet behold! suddenly one fine morning we are told that we have got to forget all that, and that we ought to interpret our position in this God's world entirely in the opposite sense. The cause which we have served, and always have been proud of serving, is suddenly declared to be a thing of evil and a menace to the country. Warfare, it appears, is against God's express commandments, is entirely opposed to human sentiments, and inevitably brings about most dreadful evil and dire misfortune. All nations, we are told, must combine against it and make its final abolition only a question of time.

PRINCE.—But surely, you must have heard some time or other, earlier in your career, voices which condemned utterly war and military service as relics of ancient barbarism?

GENERAL— Who has not? Of course I have heard them, and have read them, too, in more languages than one! But all such puny voices— you must pardon my frankness—seem to me by no means the thunderclaps that you consider them. But today matters are different; one cannot but hear these opinions, expressed as they are on all sides.

What on earth are we to do? Am I—and for that matter, every other soldier—to regard myself an honorable man, or an inhuman monster? Am I to respect myself as a willing servant in a noble cause, or am I to view my occupation with abhorrence, to repent of my misdeeds in sackcloth and ashes, and to ask pardon on my knees of every civilian for the sins of my profession?

POLITICIAN.—Why put the question so fantastically? As if anybody were asking you anything extraordinary. The new demands are addressed, not to you, but to diplomatists and other "civilians" who care precious little whether soldiers are vicious or whether they are Christ-loving. As far as you yourself are concerned, there is only one thing to be done; and that is that you should carry out unquestioningly the orders of your superiors.

GENERAL.—As you are not interested in military matters you naturally think I put the matter fantastically. You evidently don't seem to know that on certain occasions the commands of the authorities are to the effect that we act without asking for commands.

POLITICIAN. —For instance?

GENERAL.— For instance, just imagine that by the will of the powers that be I am placed in command of a whole military district. From this very fact it follows that I am commanded to govern and control in every way the troops placed in my charge. I am to develop and strengthen in them a definite point of view—to act in some definite way on their will—to influence their feelings; in a word, to educate them, so to speak, up to the purpose of their being.

Very well then. For this purpose I am empowered, amongst other things, to issue to the troops of my district general orders in my name and on my entire personal responsibility. Well, should I apply to my superior officers, asking them to dictate to me my orders, or merely to instruct in what form they should be drawn up, don't you think I should, in return, be dubbed "an old fool"? And that if it happened again, I should be summarily dismissed?

This means that I must adopt towards my troops a consistent policy, some definite spirit which, it is supposed, has been previously and once and for all approved and confirmed by the higher command. So that even to inquire about it would be to show either stupidity or impertinence. At present, however, this "definite spirit," which, as a matter of fact, has been one and the same from the times of Sargon and Assurbanipal to those of William II.—this very spirit suddenly proves to be under suspicion.

Until yesterday I knew that I had to develop and strengthen in my troops not a new, but this same old *fighting* spirit—the willingness of each individual soldier to conquer the enemy or to go to his death. And for this it is absolutely necessary to possess an unshaken faith in war as a holy cause. But now this faith is being deprived of its spiritual basis, the military work is losing what the learned call "its moral and religious sanction."

POLITICIAN. —That's all frightfully exaggerated. There has been no radical change in the accepted point of view. Even formerly, everyone always knew that war was evil and the less of it the better, and, on the other hand, wise people know now that it is a kind of evil which cannot yet be removed once and for all in our time. The problem is not the complete abolition of war, but its gradual limitation and isolation within certain narrow boundaries. The fundamental notion about war remains what it has always been, *i.e.,* that it is an inevitable evil, a calamity which must be endured upon extreme occasions.

GENERAL. And nothing else?

POLITICIAN.—Nothing else.

GENERAL *(springing up from his seat).*— Have you ever had occasion to refer to the Book of Saints?

POLITICIAN. —You mean in the Calendar? I've had to look up names of patron saints, the name-days of my friends and relatives.

GENERAL.—And have you remarked the sorts of saints in the Calendar?

POLITICIAN.—You mean in the calendar? Oh, yes, I have sometimes to run through a long list of names of saints in order to find the dates of certain birthdays.

GENERAL. Did you notice what saints are mentioned there?

POLITICIAN.—There are different kinds of saints.

GENERAL. But what are their callings?

POLITICIAN.—Their callings are as different as their names, I believe.

GENERAL. That is just where you are wrong. Their callings are not different.

POLITICIAN.—What? Surely *all* the saints are not military men?

GENERAL. Not all, but half of them.

POLITICIAN.—Exaggeration again!

GENERAL. —Well, we can't go over them one by one. But I affirm that the saints of our own Russian Church belong to two classes only: they are either monks of various orders, or princes. And to be a prince meant in old time to be a warrior. And we have no other saints—I mean those of the male sex. Monk or warrior—that is all.

LADY.—You forget the "innocents," don't you?

GENERAL.—I haven't forgotten them at all, but they were a sort of irregular monks. What the Cossacks are to the army, they were for monasticism. What's more, if you can find for me among the Russian saints one clergyman, or a tradesman, or deacon, or clerk, or commoner, or peasant—in a word, a man of any profession except monks and soldiers—then you may take the whole of my winnings which I may bring home from Monte Carlo next Sunday.

POLITICIAN.—Thank you. You can keep your treasure and your half of the saints. But tell me, please, what did you want to deduce from this discovery or observation of yours? Surely you don't mean to argue that only monks and soldiers can be a true example of moral life?

GENERAL.—You haven't altogether guessed my meaning. I myself have known many highly virtuous persons amongst the clergy, the bankers, the official classes, and the peasants, but the most virtuous person I can recollect was the old nurse of one of my friends. But we are not speaking of that.

My point really is — I mentioned the saints only to point out that it could hardly have been possible for so many soldiers to become saints, side by side with monks and in preference to members of every other peaceful and civic profession, were military occupations always regarded as a necessary evil—something like the liquor traffic or things even worse?

It is evident that the Christian nations, at whose instance the books of saints were actually compiled (and not only with the Russians was it so, but very much the same with other nations), not only respected the military calling, but they particularly respected it, and of all the lay professions only the military one was held fit to contribute members to the saintship. It is this view which seems to be incompatible with the modern campaign to abolish war.

POLITICIAN.—But I did not say that there is no change whatever. Some desirable change is undoubtedly taking place. It is true that the halo which crowned warriors and their wars in the eyes of the masses is fast disappearing. But matters have been tending this way for some long time.

And whom does that practically affect? The clergy perhaps, since the preparation of aureoles belongs to its department. But the clergy have got a good deal still to get rid of. What they cannot preserve literally they interpret in an allegorical sense, and, for the rest, take refuge in blessed silence and blessed forgetfulness.

PRINCE.—These modifications are already being made. In connection with my publications I have to watch our ecclesiastical literature. And I have already had the pleasure of reading in two journals that Christianity unconditionally condemns war.

GENERAL.—Surely not.

PRINCE.—Yes, I couldn't believe my eyes. But I can show it you.

POLITICIAN *(to the General).*——You see! But why should that worry you. You are men of deeds, not of fine words. Is all this merely professional selfishness and ambition on your part? If it is, it is indeed bad of you. But all the same, I repeat, that in practice all remains as before. Let it be true that the system of militarism, which now for thirty years has been an insupportable burden to everybody, is now bound to disappear. However, an army of some size must still remain. And in so far as it will be admitted that it is necessary, just so far the same fighting qualities as before will be demanded of it.

GENERAL.—Oh, now you're asking milk from a dead cow. But who is to give you the required fighting qualities, when the first fighting quality, without which all others are of little use, is a cheerful and confident spirit, itself the outcome of faith in the sacredness of the cause to which one has devoted oneself? And this faith cannot remain, once it is held that war is an evil and a calamity only tolerated on extreme occasions.

POLITICIAN.—Oh, we shall not ask military men to hold that opinion. Let them consider themselves the first men in the world—whose business is it? Didn't I say that Prince Luzinian was permitted to call himself King of Cyprus as long as he didn't ask us to provide him with money to buy Cyprus wine? So if you do not raid our pockets more than is necessary you may regard yourselves the salt of the earth and the flower of mankind—nobody will stop you.

GENERAL.—He says in our own eyes! But, surely, we are not talking on the moon. Are you going to keep soldiers in a sort of vacuum, so that no foreign influences could reach them? And this in the days of universal military service, short period of training, and cheap Press! No, the matter is only too clear. When once military service is compulsory for all and everybody, and when once in the whole of society, from such representatives of the State as yourself, for example, to the lowest, the new adverse criticism of the military profession becomes universally accepted, this view must needs be assimilated by the military men themselves.

If all, from the higher command downwards, begin to regard military service as an evil, inevitable for *the present,* then, in the first place, nobody will ever of his own accord choose the military calling for his life's work, with the exception perhaps of the dregs of society, which can find no other career open to it; and, secondly, all those who will be compelled to bear temporarily the military levy will do so with feelings similar to those with which criminals, chained to wheelbarrows, carry their fetters. Talk of fighting qualities and fighting spirit under such conditions! What drivel!

MR. Z.— I have always believed that after the introduction of universal military service, the abolition of armies, and eventually of individual States, is only a question of time, and that not far removed from the present moment, considering the rapid progress of events.

GENERAL.—Perhaps you're right.

PRINCE.— I think that you are *most certainly* right, though the idea has never occurred to my mind in this guise. But it is splendid! Only think: militarism creates, as its most extreme expression, the system of universal service, and then, owing to this very fact, not only modern militarism, but the very foundations of the military system as such, become utterly destroyed. Isn't it wonderful!

LADY.—Look! Even the Prince's face has brightened up. This is a pleasant change. The Prince hitherto has been wearing a gloomy countenance, which ill suited his profession of "true Christian."

PRINCE.—Yes, we are surrounded already by too many sad things; one joy remains mine, however—the knowledge of the inevitable triumph of reason over all things.

MR. Z.—There isn't the slightest doubt that militarism in Europe and in Russia will eat itself up and die of surfeit, but what sort of joys and triumphs will result from that fact remains to be seen.

PRINCE.— What? You seem to doubt that war and militarism are absolute and utter evils, of which humanity must rid itself at any cost and immediately? You doubt that complete and immediate suppression of this barbarism would *in any case* result in a triumph for reason and good?

MR. Z.— I am positively certain of quite *the opposite.*

PRINCE.— That is, of what?

MR. Z.— Of the fact that war is *not* an absolute evil, and that peace is not an absolute good; or, putting it in a simpler way, that it is possible to have—and we do have sometimes—such a thing as *a good war,* and that it is also possible to have—and we do have sometimes—an *evil peace.*

PRINCE.— Now I see the difference between your view and that held by the General: he believes, doesn't he, that war is always a good thing, and that peace is always a bad thing?

GENERAL. By no means! I understand perfectly well that sometimes war can be a very bad thing, as, for instance, was the case when we were beaten at Narva, or Austerlitz. And peace also can be a splendid thing, as, for example, the peace concluded at Nystadt, or Kuchuk–Kainardji.

LADY.—Is this a variant of the famous saying of a Kaffir or Hottentot, who told the missionary that he understood very well the difference between what is good and what is evil :—" Good is when I carry away somebody else's wives and cows, and evil is when mine are carried away from me"?

GENERAL. Don't you see that we, that is, I and your African, were only trying to say something witty: he was so unintentionally, I purposely. But now let us hear how clever people are going to discuss the question of war from the standpoint of morals.

POLITICIAN.—I would only wish that our "clever people" would not land us in casuistry and metaphysics in discussing that perfectly clear and historically–limited problem.

PRINCE.— Clear from what point of view?

POLITICIAN.—My point of view is an ordinary one, a European one, which is being gradually assimilated by cultured people, even in other parts of the world.

PRINCE.— And its essence is, of course, that everything is considered relatively and that no absolute difference is admitted between "must" and "must not," between good and evil. Isn't it so?

MR. Z.— Pardon me. But this argument seems to me rather useless in relation to the problem we are discussing. To take myself as an instance, I fully recognize the absolute opposition between moral good and evil. At the same time, it is as perfectly clear to me that war and peace do not come within the scope of the argument; that it is quite impossible to paint war all solid black, and peace all pure white.

PRINCE.— But this involves a contradiction. If the thing which is evil in itself, as, for instance, murder, can be good in certain cases, when you are pleased to call it war, what becomes then of the absolute difference between evil and good?

MR. Z.—How simple it is for you. Every murder is an unconditional evil, war is murder; therefore war is an unconditional evil. A syllogism of the first order. But you have forgotten that both the larger and the smaller premises have yet to be demonstrated, so consequently your conclusion still hangs in the air.

POLITICIAN.—Didn't I tell you we should be landed in casuistry?

LADY.—What is it they are talking about?

POLITICIAN.—Oh, about some sort of major and minor premises.

MR. Z.—Forgive me. We shall get to the business in a moment. So you affirm that on any occasion killing, to take away another person's life, is unconditional evil?

PRINCE.—Without a doubt.

MR. Z.—And to be killed—is that an unconditional evil, or not?

PRINCE.— From the Hottentot standpoint, of course it is. But we have been discussing moral evil, and this can exist only in the actions of an intelligent being, controlled by itself, and not in what happens to that being independently of its will. It follows that to be killed is the same as to die from cholera or influenza. Not only is it not absolute evil—it is not evil at all. Socrates and the Stoics have already taught us this.

MR. Z.— Well, I cannot answer for people so ancient as those. As to your moral appreciation of murder, this seems to limp somewhat. According to you it follows that absolute evil consists in causing a person something which is not evil at all. Think what you like, but there is something lame here. However, we will leave this lameness alone lest we really land in casuistry. To sum up, in killing, the evil is not in the physical fact of a life being taken, but in the moral cause of this fact, namely, in the evil will of the one who kills. Do you agree?

PRINCE.—Of course. Without that evil will there is no murder. There is only misfortune or inadvertence.

MR. Z.—It is quite clear when the will to kill is completely absent, as for instance in the case of an unsuccessful surgical operation. But it is possible to imagine a different situation, when the will, although it has not the direct aim of taking away the life of a man, yet before the fact gives its consent to a murder, regarding it as an extreme and unavoidable measure. Would such a murder also be an absolute evil in your opinion?

PRINCE. —Yes, of course, once the will agrees to murder.

MR. Z.— You will admit, however, that there are cases in which the will, though agreeing to a murder, is at the same time not an *evil* will. The murder is consequently not an absolute evil in that case, even when looked at from this subjective side?

PRINCE.— Oh, dear me! This is something quite unintelligible. However, I think I guess what you mean: you refer to that famous case in which a father sees in a lonely place a blackguardly ruffian trying to assault his innocent (and, to enhance the effect, it is added his "little") daughter. The father, unable to protect her in any other way, kills the offender. I have heard this argument at least a thousand times.

MR. Z.— What is really remarkable is not that you have heard it a thousand times, but the fact that nobody has ever had from any one of those holding your view a sensible, or even only plausible, answer to this simple argument.

PRINCE.— And what is there in it to answer?

MR. Z.— Well, if you don't like to argue against it, will you then prove by some direct and positive method that in all cases without exception, and consequently in the case we are discussing, it is indisputably better to abstain from resisting evil by means of force, than it is to use violence, though one risk the possibility of killing a wicked and dangerous man.

PRINCE.— It is funny to ask for a *special* proof for a single case. Once you recognize that murdering generally is evil in the moral sense, it is clear that it will be evil in every single case as well.

LADY.—This sounds weak, Prince, to be sure.

MR. Z.— Very weak indeed, I should say. That it is *generally* better not to kill anybody than to kill is a truth which is not subject to argument and is accepted by everybody. It is just the individual cases that actually raise the problem. The question is: Is the general and undisputable rule, "don't kill," unreservedly *absolute* and, therefore, admitting of *no* exception whatever, in *no* individual case and in *no* circumstances; or is it such as to admit of even one exception, and, therefore, is not absolute?

PRINCE.— I cannot agree to such a formal way of approaching the problem. I don't see the use of it. Suppose I admit that in your exceptional case, purposely invented for argument's sake . . .

LADY *(reprovingly)*. Prince! Prince! What is this I hear?. . .

GENERAL *(ironically)*. Ho–ho–ho, Prince!

PRINCE *(taking no notice)*. Let us admit that in your imaginary case to kill is better than not to kill (in point of fact, of course, I refuse to admit it), but let us take it for the moment that you are right. We may even take it that your case is not imaginary, but quite real, though, as you will agree, it is extremely rare, exceptional. . . . But then we are dealing with war—with something that is general, universal. You will not say yourselves that Napoleon, or Moltke, on Skobelev were in the position in any way resembling that of a father compelled to defend his innocent little daughter from the assaults of a monster.

LADY.—That's better! Bravo, *mon prince!*

MR. Z.— A clever way, indeed, to avoid a difficult question. You will allow, me, however, to establish the connection, logical as well as historical, that exists between these two facts—the single murder and the war. For this let us take again your example, only we will strip it of the details which seem to increase, though actually they only diminish, its importance. We need not trouble ourselves about a father, or a little daughter, for with them the problem at once loses its pure ethical meaning, being transferred from the sphere of intellectual and moral consciousness into that of natural moral feelings: parental love will obviously make the father kill the villain on the spot, without any further consideration as to whether he must, or has the right to do so in the light of the higher moral ideal.

So let us take not a father, but a childless moralist, before whose eyes some feeble being, strange and unfamiliar to him, is being fiercely assaulted by a cowardly villain. Would you suggest that the moralist should fold his arms and preach the glory of virtue while the fiendish beast is torturing his victim? Do you think the moralist will not feel a moral impulse to stop that beast by force, however great the possibility, or even the probability, of killing him may appear? And should he instead permit the dastardly deed to take place to the accompaniment of his high-sounding phrases, don't you think that he would find no rest from his conscience, and would feel ashamed of himself to the verge of repulsion?

PRINCE.—It is possible that a moralist who did not believe in the reality of moral order, or who forgot that God was not in might but in right, might feel so.

LADY.—Very well said,

PRINCE.— Now, MR. Z, what will you answer to this?

MR. Z.—I answer that I should have liked it to be said still better, more directly and more simply, and more closely to the actual facts. You wanted to say, did you not, that a moralist who really believes in the justice of God must, without forcibly interfering with the villain, raise his prayers to God that He should prevent the evil deed being carried out: either by a moral miracle, by suddenly turning the Villain to the path of truth; or by a physical miracle, by an instantaneous paralysis, say, or. . .

LADY.—It could be done without paralysis. The murderer might take fright at something or be in some other way diverted from his evil intention.

MR. Z.—That's all the same, because the miracle is not in the actual happening, but in the expediency of the happening, be it in physical paralysis or in some sort of mental agitation. At any rate, the method suggested by the Prince is nothing else but a prayer for a miracle.

PRINCE.—What do you mean? Why prayer, why miracle?

MR. Z.—If not, what then?

PRINCE.— Well, if I believe that the world is governed by a beneficent and intelligent living Power, I cannot but also believe that whatever takes place in the world is in accord with that Power, that is, with the will of God.

MR. Z.— Pardon me. How old are you?

PRINCE.— Whatever do you mean by this question?

MR. Z.— Nothing offensive, I can assure you. I presume you are not less than thirty, are you?

PRINCE.— Guess higher!

MR. Z.—Then you certainly must have seen, or, if you have not seen, must have heard, or, if you have not heard, must have read in the newspapers, that evil and immoral deeds do, however, take place upon this world.

PRINCE.—Well?

MR. Z.—Well, that means that moral order or truth or the will of God is not absolutely realized upon the world . . .

POLITICIAN.—Now we are at last getting to business. If evil exists, the gods, it follows, either cannot or will not suppress it, and in both cases the gods, as omnipotent and beneficent powers, do not exist at all. 'Tis old but true!

LADY.—Oh, what awful things you are saying!

GENERAL. Talking does lead one to great discoveries. Only begin philosophising, and your feeble brain reels.

PRINCE.— A poor philosophy this! As if the will of God were bound up with *our* ideas of what is good and evil.

MR. Z.— With *some* of our ideas it is not, but with the true notion of good it is bound up most firmly. Otherwise, if God is generally indifferent to good and evil, you then utterly refute your own argument.

PRINCE.— How is that, I should like to know?

MR. Z.—Because if it's all the same for the Godhead whether a savage under the influence of brutal passion destroys a weak and delicate being, then long since the Godhead must have found nothing objectionable in the man who, under the influence of compassion, destroys the savage. You will certainly not set yourself to defend anything so absurd as that the murder of a weak and innocent being is *not* evil before God, but that the murder of a strong and evil one *is*.

PRINCE.—That seems to you absurd because you lay the emphasis in the wrong place. What is morally important is not who is killed, but who kills. You yourself called the evil-doer a savage, that is, a being without conscience or reason; and how could there be moral evil, therefore, in his actions?

LADY.—Oh, oh! What question is there of a savage in the literal sense? It's all the same as if I said to my daughter, "What stupidities you are saying, my angel!" and you began to take me to task and say "Can angels say stupidities?" What a poor argument this is!

PRINCE.— I crave your forgiveness. I understand perfectly well that the villain is called a savage only in a metaphorical sense, and that this beast has neither tail nor hoofs. But it is evident that the lack of intelligence and conscience is referred to here in its literal meaning; for it would be impossible for a man with intelligence and conscience to commit such acts.

MR. Z.— Yet another play on words! Naturally, a man acting as a beast loses his intelligence and conscience in the sense that he is no longer moved by them. But that intelligence and conscience do not speak within him at all you still have to prove. In the meanwhile, I continue to think that a bestial man differs from me and you not by the absence of intelligence and conscience, but only by his willingness to act against them, and in accord with the impulse of the beast within him. Within every one of us lurks the beast, but we usually keep him tightly chained; whilst the other man loosens the chain, only to be dragged along at the tail of the beast. He has the chain, but fails to make proper use of it.

GENERAL. Precisely. And if the Prince still disagrees with you he is hoist with his own petard! "The villain," the Prince says, "is only a beast without intelligence and conscience." Then killing him is the same as killing a wolf, or a tiger springing at a man. Why, this sort of thing is permitted even by the Society for Prevention of Cruelty to Animals!

PRINCE. —But you again forget that whatever the state of that man's mind, whether reason and conscience were in complete atrophy or whether he acted with conscious immorality, the question is not about him, but about you yourselves: your reason and conscience are not atrophied, and therefore you would not consciously disregard what they demand of you—you would not have killed that man, whatever sort of man he were.

MR. Z. —Of course I shouldn't have killed him if reason and conscience had unconditionally forbidden it. But put it to yourself that my reason and conscience advise me to act another way, and that way seems to me more reasonable and conscientious.

PRINCE.—Let us hear an example. It would be curious.

MR. Z.— We may assume first of all that intelligence and conscience know how to count, at least, up to three . . .

GENERAL. Oh ho, go on!

MR. Z.— Therefore intelligence and conscience, if they do not wish to lie to me, will not keep on telling me "two" when the actual number is "three" . . .

GENERAL (impatiently). Well?

PRINCE.— I can't see what he is driving at!

MR. Z.— Well, don't you assert that intelligence and conscience speak to me only about myself and the villain? The whole matter, according to your argument, is that I should not lay a finger on him. But in point of fact there is present also a third person—who is actually the most important of all—the victim of the wicked assault, who requires my help.

You willfully neglect her, but conscience speaks of her too, and of her even in preference to the others. And if the will of God is involved here at all, it is only in the sense that I should save the victim, sparing the villain as much as possible.

But help her I must at any cost and in any case—by persuasion, if it be possible; if not by force. And should my hands be tied, then and only then can I call to my aid that supreme resource which was suggested by you too prematurely and then too lightly cast aside—the supreme resource of Prayer, that is, by an appeal to the Divine Intelligence, which,

I am sure, can really perform miracles when they are necessary. Which of these means of help should be used depends entirely on the internal and external conditions of the incident. The only absolute thing here is, that I must help those who are wronged. This is what my conscience says.

GENERAL.—Hurrah! The enemies center is broken through.

PRINCE.— My conscience has progressed beyond this elementary stage. My conscience tells me in a case like this something more definite and concise: "Don't kill!" it says, and that is all. Moreover, I do not see that we have yet advanced an iota in this argument.

Suppose I agree with your proposition that *everybody,* even a morally cultured and truly conscientious man, could permit himself to commit a murder, acting under the influence of sympathy and having no time to consider the moral character of his action—even admitting all this, I am still utterly unable to see what could follow from this admission that would enlighten us with regard to our fundamental issue? Let me ask you again: "Did Tamerlane, or Alexander the Great, or Lord Kitchener kill and make others kill people in order to protect weak, defenseless beings from the villainous assaults that were threatening them?"

MR. Z.—This juxtaposition of Tamerlane and Alexander of Macedon promises poorly for our historical sense, but since you, for the second time, you have appealed to historical facts, , allow me to quote from history an illustration which will really help us to compare the question of the defense of a person with that of the defense of a State. The affair happened in the twelfth century, at Kiev.

The feudatory princes were even then apparently of your opinion with regard to war, and holding that quarrelling and fighting should be confined to home, they would not agree to go out to fight the Polovtsi[7], saying that they would be sorry to cause people the horrors of war. To that the Grand Duke Vladimir Monomakh made the following reply: "You are sorry for these serfs,[8] but you forget that Spring is coming. . . . The serf will go out with his horse to plough.

LADY.—Please don't use bad words!

MR. Z.— But this is from a chronicle.

LADY.—That makes no difference. I am sure you don't remember the chronicle by heart, so may just as well put it in your own words. It sounds so absurd. One hears "Spring will come" and expects "the flowers

---

[7] Kumans. The Russians called them Polovtsi. Ed.

[8] The equivalent Russian word "smerd" (serf, slave, etc.) suggests something stinking. (Tr.)

will blossom and the nightingales will sing," but instead all of a sudden comes "serf."'

MR. Z.— As you please, madam. "The spring will come, the Polovtsi will come, kill the peasant, and lead off his horse; they will come in great numbers, massacre all the peasants, carry off all the women and children, drive off the cattle and burn their homes and the village.

Can't you find it in your heart to pity the peasants for this? I do pity them, and for that reason I call upon you to take up arms against the Polovtsi."

On that occasion the princes were put to shame, and the land had protection throughout the rule of Vladimir Monomakh. But they afterwards returned to their peace–loving state, which urged them to evade war with foreign enemies in order that they could carry 'on in comfort their miserable quarrels in their own homes. The end of it all for Russia was the Mongolian yoke, and for the descendants of these princes that rich feast of experience which history provided them in the person of Ivan the Terrible.

PRINCE.—This is all beyond me. You cite an event which never occurred to any of us, and certainly never will occur, and call up some Vladimir Monomakh, who perhaps never existed at all, and with whom, at any rate, has absolutely nothing to do with us. . . .

LADY.—Parlez tour vous, monsieur.

MR. Z.— Tell me, Prince, are you a descendant of Rurik?

PRINCE.—They say so, but what interest to me, do you think, are Rurik, Sineus, and Truvor?[9]

LADY.—I think when one does not know one's ancestors one is little better than the little boys and girls who believe that they were found in the garden under a cabbage–leaf.

PRINCE.—And what about those poor devils who don't happen to have any ancestors?

MR. Z.— Everybody has at least two great ancestors, who have bequeathed to posterity their circumstantial and highly instructive records: the history of one's country and that of the world.

PRINCE.—But these memoirs cannot determine for us the question what are we to be now, what ought we to do now. Let it be granted that

---

[9] The legendary founders of the Russian State. (Tr.)

Vladimir Monomakh did exist, and was not simply the imagination of the monk Laurentius, or the monk Hypathius. I admit even that he was an exceptionally good man and may have sincerely pitied the "serfs," in any case he was right to fight with the Polovtsi, because in those wild times moral conscience had not triumphed over the coarse Byzantine notion of Christianity, and it actually approved of man-killing when it was for a good purpose, real or imaginary.

But how can we do so, once we have understood that murder is an evil, something contrary to the will of God, forbidden since the days of Moses by God's commandment? When we know that it cannot be permitted us under any guise, under any name, and cannot cease to be evil when instead of being the killing of one it becomes the killing of thousands under the name of war? It is first of all a question of personal conscience.

GENERAL.—Well, if it is a matter of personal conscience, permit me to make the following personal report. I am a man who in the moral sense, as of course in most other senses, am altogether average —neither black nor white, but grey. I have not evinced either special virtue or special sin. But in all good acts there is always a difficulty in weighing their merit; you can never be sure whether your conscience had been obeyed, whether your conscience stands for real good or only for a kind of mental softness, a habit of life, or an impulse of vanity.

Good acts always seem to be in a small petty way. In the whole of my life I only remember one good occasion which it would be impossible to name petty, but I know absolutely that then there was no doubt whatever about my impulse; I acted solely at the dictates of a good power. It was the one occasion in life when I experienced a complete moral satisfaction, where I fell even into a sort of ecstasy because I had acted without reflection or hesitation.

My act remains till now, and will of course remain for ever, my purest memory. Well, and that one good act of mine was a murder, and not by any means a small murder, for in a quarter of an hour I killed considerably more than a thousand men.

LADY.—What rubbish! And I thought that you were—serious.

GENERAL—Altogether serious; I could bring witnesses. Certainly I did not kill with my hands, with these sinful hands, but with the aid of six pure, chaste, steel cannon, with the most virtuous and beneficial shrapnel.

LADY.—What good was there in that?

GENERAL.—Well, of course, although I am a military man, and, even according to our present style, a militarist, I should not call the simple destruction of a few thousands of ordinary people something good, be they Germans or Hungarians or Englishmen or Turks. This was something quite special. I cannot even now speak about it with equanimity. It stirred up my soul so much.

LADY.—Well, don't keep us in suspense, tell us it quickly.

GENERAL.—Since I mentioned the cannon, you no doubt guess that it was in the last Turkish war. I was in the Third Caucasian Army. After the third of October . . .

LADY.—What about October 3rd?

GENERAL.—That was when the fight on the heights of Aladzhin took place, when we for the first time broke up the flanks of the "invincible" Gazi–Mukhtar Pasha. . . . Well, after the third of October we began our advance. I was commander of the advance reconnoitering division; I had the Nizhni Novgorod dragoons, three hundred Kuban Cossacks and a battery of horse artillery. It was a dreary country, not bad up in the mountains, beautiful, but down in the valleys nothing but deserted, burnt-out villages and downtrodden fields were to be seen.

One morning—October the 28th, it was—we were descending a valley, where according to the map there was a big Armenian village. As a matter of fact there was no village to be seen, though there had really been one there not long before, and of a decent size, too: its smoke could be seen miles away.

I had my detachment well together in close formation, for reports had been received that we might run into a strong cavalry force. I was riding with the dragoons; the Cossacks were in advance.

Quite close to the village the road had a sharp turn. The Cossacks galloped round, suddenly they reined in their horses and then came to a full stop, as if rooted to the earth. I galloped up to them, but before I saw with my own eyes I guessed from the smell what was the matter.

Before I could see anything I guessed by the smell of roasting flesh that the Bashi-Bazouks[10] had left their "kitchen" behind. A huge caravan of Armenian refugees had not been able to escape in time. The crowd had been caught by the Turks, who had "made a good job of it" in their own inimitable fashion. They had bound the poor Armenians, some by the

---

[10] Irregular soldiers of the Ottoman Army notorious for being brutal and undisciplined. Ed.

head, some by the feet, some by the waist, to the high cart axles, had lit fires underneath, and had slowly grilled them.

Dead women lay here and there—some with breasts cut off, others with abdomens ripped open. I need not go into further particulars. But one scene will remain for ever vivid in my memory. A poor woman lay there on the ground, her head and shoulders securely bound to the cart's axle, so that she could not move her head. She bore no burns, no wounds. But on her distorted face was stamped a ghastly terror—she had evidently died of sheer horror. And before her dead, staring eyes was a high pole, firmly fixed in the ground, and to it was tied the poor little naked body of a baby—her son, most likely—a blackened, scorched little corpse, with eyes that protruded. Near by also was a grating in which lay the dead ashes of a fire. . . . I was completely overcome with the ghastliness of the thing.

Such a mortal sorrow overcame me that I looked upon God's earth with loathing and I could not reason—my actions became mechanical. Grimly I bade my men put their horses to the gallop. We entered the burned village; it was razed to the ground; there was not one stone left upon another.

Suddenly we saw what seemed like a scarecrow emerging from a dry well . . . all muddy and torn, he came up to us, fell flat on the ground, and began wailing something in Armenian. We helped him to his feet, and plied him with eager questions. He was a little, intelligent fellow; he had just arrived at this village on business when the inhabitants were beginning to flee. They had hardly started off when the Bashi–Bazouks fell upon them —an immense number, he said—at least forty thousand. He managed to hide himself in the well. He heard the cries of the tortured people; he knew full well what was happening.

Later, he heard the Bashi–Bazouks come back and and gallop off again by a different route. "They were going to my own village," he groaned, "and then they will do the same terrible things to all our folk." The poor wretch moaned pitifully, wringing his hands in despair. At that moment an inspiration seemed suddenly to come to me. My agony of soul seemed suddenly comforted, it was as if a light had suddenly shone in my soul. My heart melted, and God's world again smiled before me. "Have they long gone?" I said to the Armenian. He reckoned it about three hours.

When I heard that it was as if a light had suddenly shone in my soul. My heart melted, and God's world again smiled before me. "Have they long gone?" I said to the Armenian. He reckoned—three hours.

Well, we couldn't make up three hours' difference in so short a space, that was certain. "Oh, Lord! "said I, "isn't there another road, a shorter one?"

"I do, sir, I do." And he became at once excited." There is a way across the defile. It is very short. And only very few people know it."

"Is it passable on horseback?"

"It is, sir."

"And for artillery?"

" It would be rather difficult, but it could be done, sir."

We gave the Armenian a horse, and with the whole detachment followed him into the defile. How we climbed among the mountains I hardly remember. Once more I felt like a machine, though there was in my soul a lightness as if I lay on feathers. I had complete assurance. I knew what was necessary to do, and I felt what would be done.

We were just issuing from the last neck of the defile when suddenly our Armenian gallops back, waving his arms and crying, "There they are; there they are!" I caught up with the advance guard, and leveling my telescope I could see that he was right. I saw an apparently endless column of horses—not forty thousand, of course, but three or four thousand at least, if not even five.

These sons of devils at once spotted the Cossacks and turned to meet them. We were coming out of the defile against their left front. A hail of bullets greeted the Cossacks. These Asiatic monsters could fire their European guns as if they were really human beings. Here and there a Cossack was picked off by a shot. A Cossack officer rode up to me and shouted: "Order the attack, sir. Why should these beasts be allowed to shoot us like quails, while we are mounting our artillery? We can put them to flight ourselves."

"Patience, my dear fellow, for just one little moment," I told him." I have no doubt that you would be able to put them to flight; but what would be the pleasure of that? God bids me wipe them out and not drive them away."

Well, I ordered an advance of 200 Cossacks in open formation, and they engaged the enemy, exchanging some volleys with them. We kept a hundred of the men back to mask the artillery, and placed the Nizhni Novgorods in the recesses to the left of the battery. I myself trembled all the while with impatience. The face of that burnt child with the protruding eyes was constantly before me. The Cossacks were falling, shot! God! what an agony of suspense. . . .

LADY.—How did it end?

GENERAL.—It ended in the best way possible. The Cossacks began to retreat, crying their Cossack cries the while. Those sons of devils came pell–mell after them, too excited even to fire, and galloping *en masse* on our position. When they were within 400 yards of our line the Cossacks suddenly scattered, all in different directions, each man seeking cover where he could. "At last," I saw that "the hour of God's will had arrived." I turned to the squad of Cossacks covering the guns. "Cossacks! wheel!" I shouted. The covering squad divided, right and left, leaving the battery unmasked. One fierce prayer to God, "All is in order; God give us His blessing!" said I to myself, and then I gave the word "Fire!"

And God blessed all my six cannon. The first round put them in confusion, the whole horde turned to flight. The swine did not come to their senses even when the second volley of shells smote them, cutting red lanes through and through. Suddenly the horde wheeled. A third volley followed them up! What a bloody mess it made! Have you seen an ants' nest, on which burning matches have been thrown?—the ants all rushing about, crushing each other? . . . They went off with a rush in all directions, in many cases trampling one another down.

Then our Cossacks and dragoons of the left flank went after them cutting, hacking, and slicing them like cabbage. Those who escaped the artillery perished on their swords. Many threw down their arms, leapt from their saddles, and offered themselves as hostages. Some whined for mercy. But I was past giving orders. My men understood well enough that it was not a time for mercy. So the Cossacks and the men of Nijny–Novgorod sabred them to a man.

And if only these brainless Satans had not taken fright at our fire, and instead of running away when they were between forty and sixty yards from us had flung themselves upon us and taken the cannon, we would had never given them a third round.

Well, God was with us! The business was done, and it was Easter–day in my soul, the bright day of the resurrection of Christ. We gathered our dead, thirty–seven men who had given their souls to God. We placed them on a level stretch of land in several rows, and closed their eyes. There was among us in the third hundred an old sargeant, Odarchenko, a well–read man of remarkable capacity. In England he would have become Prime Minister. Now he's in Siberia for personal opposition to the authorities when they were closing some monastery of the Old

Believers and destroying the grave of a much venerated elder of the sect. I called him:

"Now, Odarchenko," said I, "that we are in the field there is no time for arguing about the right alleluias; so you be our priest and sing the requiem for our dead." For him that was a pleasure of the first order.

"I shall be glad to do it, Sir," says he, his face all shining. For him this was, of course, a Heaven–sent opportunity. We also found our rough–and–ready choir for the service. We sang the departing souls away with full rites. Only the absolution was lacking, but this was not necessary either: their sins were already remitted by the words of Christ himself about those who "lay down their lives for their friends." Even now I can see the ceremony vividly before my eyes.

The day had been a cloudy autumn one, but before sunset the heavy clouds disappeared. The gorge was black beneath us, but in the sky the light cloudlets were of many colors, as if the regiments of God were gathering. My soul was still in ecstasy with the glory of our fight. Wondrous peace rested upon me; I felt that all worldly stains were washed away, and that all the burden of earthly trouble had fallen from my shoulders.

I was in Paradise—I was feeling God, and there was the end of it. And as Odarchenko called out the names of the newly departed warriors who had sacrificed their lives on the field of battle for faith and Tsar and their country, I truly felt that the official title given them was not merely an official verbosity, but they were indeed a Christ–serving army, and that war, as it was, so it is and will be to the end of the world, a great honorable and holy doing . . .

PRINCE (*after a short silence*).— Well, when you buried your men in your happy frame of mind, tell me, didn't you think at all of the enemies whom you had killed in such great numbers?

GENERAL.—No, glory be to God! We managed to move a little further back so that that carrion did not remind us of its presence.

LADY.—Ah, now you've spoilt the whole impression. How could you?

GENERAL (*turning to the Prince*).—And what would you personally have wished of me? That I should give Christian burial to these jackals who were neither Christian nor Muslims, but devil knows what? If I had gone out of my mind, and had indeed ordered that they be buried together with our Cossacks in one funeral service, you would very probably have convicted me of religious assault. How, man?

You actually subject these dear unfortunates, who in their lifetime worshipped the devil, to a superstitious and coarse pseudo-Christian ritual! No, I had something else to do, I gave orders and made a manifesto to the effect that none of the people approach within ten yards of this devil's carrion, for I saw that my Cossacks' fingers had long since been itching to search their pockets according to custom. And who knew what plague might have been let loose on us! It might have been the death of us all.

PRINCE.—Have I then understood you aright? You were afraid, lest the Cossacks going to rob the bodies of the Bashi-Bazouks should carry infection into your camp?

GENERAL.—Yes, that's just what I was afraid of. It seems clear.

PRINCE.—There's your Christ-serving army!

GENERAL.—The Cossacks, eh? . . . They are veritable brigands! Always were and always will be.

PRINCE.— But, really, what is all this? Are we talking in dreams?

GENERAL.—Yes, it seems to me that there must be something wrong. I can't make out what it is that you really want to know.

POLITICIAN.—The Prince is probably astonished that your ideal, all but canonized Cossacks, suddenly appear to be, in your own words, brigands.

PRINCE.—Yes, and I ask in what way can war be a great, honorable and holy doing when all it comes to, even by your own showing, a struggle of one set of robbers with another.

GENERAL.—Eh! So that's what you were after. "A struggle of one set of brigands against another." Yes, there is something in what you say. I agree that it is with another set of robbers, with an altogether other set. Or do you in sober reality think that to steal when you have the chance is the same sort of thing as to roast little babies before the eyes of their mothers?

Now this is what I say to you. My conscience is so clear about this affair that I sometimes am sorry from the depths of my heart that I did not die at the moment when I gave the order for the last volley. I have not the slightest doubt that dying then I should have gone straight with my thirty-seven Cossacks to the Throne of God, and we should have taken our places in Paradise side by side with the repentant thief of the Gospel. It was not for nothing that the Bible placed him there, was it?

PRINCE.— That is true. But you will certainly not find it written in the Bible that only people of our own country or of our own religion can be likened to the Penitent Thief, and not people of all nationalities and creeds.

GENERAL.— Upon my word, you could not place more misstatements to my credit if I were already dead! When did I make any distinction of nationality or religion in this business? Are the Armenians my fellow–countrymen or fellow–Churchmen, or did I ask of what faith were this devil's brood which I destroyed with our artillery?

PRINCE.—However, you do not seem to have been able to recollect that this same devil's brood were all the same, human beings, and that in every man there is a sense of good and evil, and that every robber, be he Cossack or Bashi–Bazouk, might prove to be the repentant thief of the Gospel.

GENERAL.—Have done with all that! First you say that an evil man is in nature like an irresponsible beast, then you say that the Bashi–Bazouk roasting a baby might turn out to be the penitent thief of the Gospel! And all because you fear to touch evil even with one finger! But according to my lights, what is important is not that in every man are the roots of good and evil, but which of the two prevails.

It is not so interesting that out of every kind of grape–juice it is possible to make both wine and vinegar as to know what actually is in that bottle there, wine or vinegar. Because if it is vinegar and I begin to drink it by tumbler fulls and to offer it to others under the pretext that it is made from one and the same material as wine, I shall certainly help no one by that wisdom, unless spoiling their stomachs is any help.

All people are brothers. Splendid! Very glad to hear it! But how far will this take us? There are different kinds of brothers, you know. And why not be interested to know which of my brothers is Cain and which Abel? And if before my eyes my brother Cain fall upon my brother Abel, and I then through lack of equanimity give brother Cain such a box on the ear that he's not likely to do it again,—you suddenly reproach me that I have forgotten to be brotherly. I perfectly well remember why I interfered, and if I had not remembered I could quite calmly have passed by on the other side.

PRINCE.—But why those alternatives—either passing by or dealing a blow?

GENERAL.-A third way you seldom find on such occasions. You have proposed prayer to God for His direct interference, that He should instantly, and with His strong right arm, bring each devil's son to reason.

But you yourself cast this idea aside, didn't you? I admit willingly that prayer is good in all circumstances, but it cannot be substituted for action on one's own part. Pious folk say grace before dinner, but they chew with their own jaws. It was not without prayer that I gave the orders to the artillery.

PRINCE.—Such a prayer is, of course, blasphemy. It is necessary not so much to pray to God as to act according to the will of God.

GENERAL.—For instance?

PRINCE.—A man who is filled with the true spirit of the Gospel will find in himself, when necessary, the power, with words and gestures and with his whole appearance to act upon the mind of his unfortunate dark brother who wishes to commit a murder or some other evil,—he will be able to make on him such a startling impression that he will at once understand his mistake and turn away from the ways of evil.

GENERAL.—Holy martyrs! Do you mean to say that I should have gone forward to the Bashi–Bazouks who murdered the babies, and made touching gestures and said touching words?

MR. Z.—Words, owing to the distance and to your mutual ignorance of one another's language, would, I imagine, have been completely out of place. And as far as gestures go in making a staggering impression, as you will of course, but I should have thought that under the given circumstances one couldn't think of anything better than a volley or so of shells.

LADY.—But really, do tell us, Prince, in what language and by the help of what instruments could the General have explained himself to the Bashi–Bazouks?

PRINCE.— I have never said that the General could have impressed the Bashi–Bazouks in the Christian way. What I did say was that a man full of the true Christian spirit would have found some means, in this case as in every other, to awaken in those dark souls the good which lies hidden in every human being.

MR. Z.—You really think so?

PRINCE.—I do not doubt it in the least.

MR. Z.—Well, do you think that Christ was *sufficiently* imbued with the true spirit of the Gospel, or no?

PRINCE. —What a strange question to ask?

MR. Z.—Well, this is what I'd like to know: why did not Christ bring the evangelical spirit to bear in such a way upon the souls of Judas, Herod, the Jewish Sanhedrin, and the *impenitent* thief, who usually remains entirely for gotten when they speak of his penitent companion?

Why did He not bring out the good in them? From a positive Christian point there is no insurmountable difficulty in it. But you have got to give up one of two things: either your habit of taking refuge with Christ and the Gospel as with the highest authority, or your moral optimism, because the third way, the well–worn way, of denying the evangelical fact itself as a modern fiction or priestly interpretation, is in the present instance completely closed to you.

However much you mutilate and ransack the four Gospels for texts, the principal fact from the point of view of our question will remain indisputable, and that is, that Christ Himself suffered bitter persecution and death because of the malice of His enemies. That He Himself remained morally higher than all that malice, that He did not wish to offer any opposition, and that He forgave His enemies, is as comprehensible from my point of view as from yours.

But why did He not,—using your words— forgiving His enemies, deliver their souls from that dreadful darkness in which they then were? Why did He not overcome their malice by the force of His own sweetness? Why did He not awaken the sleeping good in them? Why did He not give them light and new spiritual birth?

In a word, why did He not act upon Judas, Herod, and the Jewish Sanhedrin in the same way as He acted upon the one repentant thief? Either He could not or He would not. In both cases, however, according to your argument, Christ must have been insufficiently imbued with the true Christian spirit! On which conclusion I beg you to accept my hearty congratulations.

PRINCE.—Oh, I am not going to enter into verbal fencing with you any more than I am going to enter into real fencing with the General, with "Christ–serving" swords . . .

(At this point the Prince got up from his seat and wished apparently to say something very powerful, expecting with one blow, without any fencing, to overwhelm his antagonist, but at that moment the bells of a neighboring church began to strike seven.)

LADY. —Dinner–time! But a discussion like this should not be finished hurriedly. After dinner we play whist, but tomorrow this conversation must certainly be continued. *(To the Politician)* You agree?

POLITICIAN.—What, to continue this conversation? I was overjoyed that it had come to an end! The dispute had taken the rather unpleasant complexion of a religious controversy! It was too hot a work for this time of the year. My health I can tell you, is dearer to me than any of these things.

LADY.—Don't pretend! You must, you absolutely must, take part. You ought to be ashamed of yourself—lounging there stretched out on your deck chair like a mysterious Mephistopheles.

POLITICIAN.—Very well, I might agree to take part tomorrow, but only on condition that religion be left out of it as much as possible. I don't ask you to exclude it altogether, as it seems that would be impossible. Only let there be less, for God's sake, as little of it as possible!

LADY.—Your "for God's sake" is on this occasion very sweet.

MR. Z. *(to the Politician).*—The best means of making sure that there shall be less religion would be for you to monopolize the conversation, wouldn't it?

POLITICIAN.—I will I promise you. Only to listen is, all the same, more pleasant than to talk, especially in this fine air; but for the salvation of our little circle from mutual conflict, which might possibly reflect itself in an unpleasant way upon our whist, I am ready to sacrifice myself for two hours.

LADY.—Splendid And the day after tomorrow then, we will finish this discussion about the Bible. The Prince will get ready some absolutely irrefutable argument. Only you also must be present at the end. But you must be ready too. After all, one should learn at least a little of matters ecclesiastical!

POLITICIAN.—What! The day after tomorrow, as well? No, no! My self-sacrifice won't go as far as that. What's more, I must go to Nice the day after tomorrow.

LADY.—To Nice? What a transparent pretext! It's no good. We've long since seen through you. Now everybody knows that when you say you're going to Nice it means you're off to Monte Carlo for a spree. Never mind, we'll manage somehow without you. Go and wallow in pleasure, since you're not afraid of the fact that you will have to join the world of spirits later on. Go to Monte Carlo, and may Providence reward you according to your deserts!

POLITICIAN.— My deserts don't concern *Providence*, as it happens, but only the *provision* a certain necessary business which I have got to see through. I might try my luck with a little small change at roulette, I admit, but I shouldn't spend much.

LADY.— Tomorrow, then, we must all be present.

SECOND DISCUSSION
"Audiatur et altera *pars."*

ON the following day, at the appointed hour, I met the others at afternoon tea under the palm trees. Only the Prince was absent. We had to wait for him. As I did not play cards I wrote down the whole of this conversation from the very beginning. This time the Politician spoke so much and in such a drawling way that to note down literally everything he said would be impossible. I have mentioned a sufficient number of his remarks and have endeavored to preserve the general meaning. In many instances I can merely convey in my own words the substance of his discourses.

POLITICIAN.—I have long observed a certain peculiarity: people who have made a special hobby of some kind of higher morality cannot master the simplest and most indispensable, and according to me, the most necessary virtue—common politeness. We must therefore be grateful to God that in our midst there are comparatively few possessed of this notion of higher morality. I say *notion* advisedly, because in reality I have never met with it, nor do I believe in its existence.

LADY.—Well, that is not new, but what you say about politeness is true. Try, before you have come to the subject in question, to prove that politeness is the only indispensable virtue; try to prove it even superficially, as musical instruments are tuned before the overture begins.

POLITICIAN.— When the orchestra is tuning up, we hear only single disconnected sounds. I fear my proof would inflict on us a similar monotony; for hardly anybody would urge the opposite opinion—at least, not before the Prince comes in. Of course, when he arrives it would not be polite at all to speak of politeness.

LADY.—Certainly. But what are your arguments?

POLITICIAN.—This, I think you will agree that one can exist quite well in a society where there are no chaste, disinterested or unselfish persons. I, at any rate, have got on very well in such company.

LADY.—At Monte Carlo!

POLITICIAN. —At Monte Carlo and everywhere else. In fact, nowhere is there felt to be a demand for even a single representative of the higher virtues. But try to live in a society where there is not a single polite person.

GENERAL.—I do not know to what society you are good enough to refer, but during the campaigns[11] in Khiva and Turkey something more than politeness was needed.

POLITICIAN.—You might as well have added that for travelers in Central Africa more than politeness was required. I speak of well–organized daily life in a civilized human society, and that requires none of the higher virtues or of Christianity so–called. *(Turning to Mr. Z.)* You shake your head.

MR. Z.—I recall to mind a painful incident which was told me.

LADY.—And what was that?

MR. Z.—My friend N. died quite suddenly.

GENERAL.—The well–known novelist?

MR. Z.—The same.

POLITICIAN.—The newspapers wrote rather mysteriously about his death.

MR. Z.—Precisely—very mysteriously.

LADY. —But what made you think of him just now? Did he die from somebody's lack of politeness?

MR. Z.—On the contrary, he died through his own excessive politeness and through nothing else.

GENERAL. —Once more, it seems, it is impossible for us to agree.

LADY.— Tell us the story, please, if you can.

MR. Z.—There is nothing to hide. My friend, who also thought that politeness, although not the only virtue, was, at all events, the most necessary step in social morality, considered it his bounden duty to fulfill all its dictates. Among the duties which he imposed on himself was that of reading all letters addressed to him, even from unknown people, as well as books and pamphlets for review. He read all the letters and noticed all the books. He conscientiously carried out every request addressed to him, and consequently was busy all day with other people's affairs, while his own occupied him at night.

---

[11] A play upon words in Russian; the word for "company" stands also for "campaign." (Tr.)

What is more, he accepted all invitations and received all comers. While my friend was young and could stand strong drinks the hard labor imposed by politeness, although undermining his health, did not degenerate into tragedy. Wine cheered his heart and saved him from despair. Sometimes, when ready to seize a rope with which to hang himself, he stretched out his hand for the bottle, and that gave him courage. Constitutionally he was weak, and at the age of forty-five he had to give up strong drink. When sober, this slavery seemed hell to him, and now, I am informed, he has committed suicide.

LADY.—What! And simply from politeness? But he was mad!

MR. Z.— I have no doubt that the poor fellow had lost his spiritual and mental balance. But the word "simply" I think is hardly applicable to his case.

GENERAL.—I have also seen similar cases of insanity, and if one tried to fathom them one might also go mad. It is far from simple.

POLITICIAN.—In every case it is clear that politeness has nothing to do with the matter. The Spanish throne was no more to blame for the madness of the Councilor Popristchin[12] than the necessity to be polite was answerable for your friend's insanity.

MR. Z.— I quite agree. I am by no means opposed to politeness, I merely object to making any kind of absolute rule.

POLITICIAN.—Absolute rules, as everything absolute, are merely the inventions of people bereft of common sense and of the feeling of living reality. I do not admit any absolute rules, I only accept *necessary* rules. For instance, I am well aware that if I do not adopt the rule of cleanliness the result will be unpleasant to myself and to others. In order not to experience unpleasant sensations, I adhere unalterably to the rule of washing myself every day, to putting on clean linen, etc., not because it is a generally received custom of other people or myself, or because it is a sacred duty, or a sin to neglect it, but merely because uncleanliness, *ipso facto,* is a material inconvenience. Just the same applies to politeness, of which cleanliness is a component part. For me and for others it is much more *convenient* to perform than to neglect the rules of politeness, and therefore I adhere to them. Your friend imagined that politeness meant answering all letters and executing all requests without reference to convenience and personal advantage; that was not politeness, but a kind of foolish self-sacrifice.

---

[12] The hero in Gogol's "Diary of a Madman."

MR. Z.—Morbid development of conscientiousness became, in his case, a mania, which killed him.

LADY.—But it is awful that a man should perish through such nonsense. Could not you bring him to his senses?

MR. Z.—I did my best, and was even powerfully assisted by a pilgrim from Mount Athos, who was half crazy himself, but a very remarkable person. My friend greatly respected him and often consulted him in spiritual matters. The pilgrim instantly perceived the root of all the trouble. I knew the pilgrim well and was sometimes present at the discussions.

When my friend began telling him about his moral doubts, saying—was he right in this or had he sinned in that, Varsonophius would immediately interrupt him: "What! Are you distressed about your sins—don't! Listen to me: sin five hundred and thirty-nine times in a day, but don't grieve about it; that's the chief thing.

If to sin is evil, then to remember sin is evil. There is nothing worse than to call to mind one's own sins. Better think of the evil which others do to you, there is some use in that; for the future you will beware of such persons. As for your evil actions—forget them, so that they may disappear altogether. There is only one mortal sin and that is despondency. From despondency comes despair; and that is more than sin, it is spiritual death.

Well, and what other sins are there? How about drunkenness? A sensible man drinks when he is thirsty; he does not drink at random, but a fool gorges himself even with plain water, therefore the evil is not in the wine, but in the foolishness.

Some people in their foolishness burn their insides with *vodka,* and even their outsides turn black and little flashes of blue flame flicker all over them. I have seen it with my own eyes. Now, how can you speak of the presence of sin when all the time hell itself is visibly coming out from you?

And as to transgressions of the seventh commandment, let me tell you candidly that it is as difficult to censure them as it is impossible to praise them. But I can hardly recommend them! There is ecstatic pleasure in it—one cannot deny it—but at the end it brings despondency and shortens one's life. If you don't believe me, see what a learned German doctor writes."

And Varsonophius took an antiquated-looking book from the shelf and began turning over its leaves. "Here is Hufland. See page 176." And he would slowly read passages in which the German author earnestly warns his readers against extravagant waste of the vital forces.

"Well, you see, why should a reasonable man exhaust his strength? In early, reckless years evil is done and health is lost. But to recall all the past and be distressed, saying why did I lose my innocence, my purity of soul and body! Well, this, I can assure you, is mere foolishness. It simply means that you deliver yourself right into the hands of the Devil for his eternal amusement. It flatters him, naturally, that your soul cannot go forward and upward, but stays marking time in the same old filthy spot.

But here is my advice to you: as soon as he starts disturbing you by this sort of repentance, you simply spit and rub it with your foot, saying, 'See now, all my grievous sins, here they are. Ah, what a lot they mean to me. What rot!' I can assure you he will leave you alone—I speak from experience. . . . Well, what other sins have you got? Are you thinking of trying stealing? And if you did steal—there is no very great harm in it: nowadays everybody steals. Therefore, you mustn't think anything of such a trifle at all.

The one thing to beware of is despondency. When thoughts come about sins—have not I wronged or offended some one?— go to the theater, or to some merry friends, or read some funny stories. And if a rule is wanted, here it is: be firm in your faith, not from fear of sin, but because it is a joyful thing for a wise man to live with God; without God a man is utterly wretched.

Study the word of God, for if you read it carefully there is comfort and happiness in every verse. Say your prayers with real uplifting of your soul once or twice every day. You never by any chance forget to wash yourself? No? Well, a sincere prayer is better for a man's soul than any amount of soap is for his body. Fast for the health of the stomach and your other organs. Just now every doctor is prescribing this for people on the wrong side of forty.

Don't worry about other people's business, and don't go in for organized charity, if you have your own occupation. But give alms to the poor you meet, and never stay to count the cost. Give without stint to churches and monasteries. Do not reckon the amount; in Heaven's clearing–house they will count it all up themselves. And then, you will be healthy in body and soul, and as for those hypocrites who would poke their noses into everybody's soul, because they find their own so hollow—with these you must never even speak."

Such talks as these had a very good effect on my poor friend, but even they could not at the last raise him from the mire of despondency; besides, lately he seldom met Varsanophius.

POLITICIAN.—The pilgrim says, in substance, pretty much what I have been saying.

LADY. So much the better. But what a wonderful moralist he is, indeed! "Sin, if you must, but above all never repent." It appeals to me mightily!

GENERAL.—I presume he does not say the same to everybody. If it were a murderer or a scoundrel I suppose he would give some different teaching.

MR. Z.—Well, of course. But when he meets a man overwhelmed with moral doubts he at once becomes a philosopher and even a fatalist. A very clever and well-educated old lady was delighted with him. Although of the Russian orthodox faith, she had been educated abroad.

She heard much about Varsonophius and consulted him as though he were a *directeur de conscience.*[13] He, however, did not let her talk much about the worries of her soul. "And why do you worry yourself about all this rubbish? Who wants to hear it? I am only a common peasant, and yet it bores me to death. How can you imagine, then, that God can take any interest in it? And what is there to talk about! You are too old and too weak to begin improvement now."

She afterwards herself told me this conversation, laughing and weeping at the same time. True, she tried to argue with him, but he completely persuaded her by a story from the life of two ancient hermits—Varsanophius narrated it to me and N. very often. It is a very fine story, only it will perhaps take too long to tell it.

LADY.—But tell it to us in a few words.

MR. Z.—I will try. In the desert of Nitria two hermits were "working out" their salvation. Their caves were not far from each other, but they never conversed, only chanted psalms occasionally. Thus they passed many years, and their fame began to spread through Egypt and the surrounding countries.

It came to pass that one day the Devil managed to put into their minds, both at the same time, one and the same desire, and without saying a word to each other they collected their work, baskets and mats made of palm leaves and branches, and went off to Alexandria. They sold their work there, and then for three days and three nights they sought pleasure in the company of drunkards and libertines, after which they went back to their desert.

---

[13] Spiritual advisor. Ed.

And one of them lamented and cried out in bitterness and agony of soul: "I am lost eternally! Cursed am I! For no prayers and penance can atone for such madness, such abominations! All my years of fastings, vigils and prayers are wasted! I am ruined, body and soul!"

The other man walked beside him and sang psalms joyfully to himself. "Brother," said the repentant one, "have you gone mad?"

"Why do you ask that?" asked the joyful one.

"Aren't you sorry?"

"About what should I be sorry?"

"Listen to him! Have you forgotten Alexandria?"

"Glory be to God, who preserves the famous and God–fearing city."

"And what did we do at Alexandria?"

"You know well enough yourself; we sold our baskets, bowed low to St. Mark and visited the other churches; we called on the pious governor of the city, conversed with the good prioress Leonilla, who is always kind to monks. . . . . . ."

"But didn't we spend the night in a house of ill fame?"

"God save us! No! We spent the evening and night in the patriarch's court."

"Holy martyrs! He has lost his mind. . . Where then did we treat ourselves to wine?"

"We partook of wine and food at the patriarch's table on the occasion of the Presentation of the Blessed Virgin in the Temple."

"Poor, miserable creature! And who was it whom we kissed, not to mention worse things. . ."

"We were honored with a holy kiss on departing by the Father of Fathers, the most blessed archbishop of the great city of Alexandria and the whole of Egypt, Libya and Pentapolis,[14] and judge of the World, Cyrus–Timotheus, with all the fathers and brothers of his God–chosen clergy.."

"But are you mocking me? Or is it that the Devil himself has entered your soul as punishment for the abominations of yesterday? They were wretched libertines, you scoundrel, that you kissed!"

---

[14] Cyrenaica. Ed.

"Well, I don't know which of us the Devil has entered: whether he has entered me, who am rejoicing in the gifts of God and in the benevolence of the godly priests, and am praising my Maker, as should every other living thing—or whether he has entered you, who are now raving like a madman and calling the house of our blessed father and pastor a house of ill fame, all the time insulting him and his God–loved clergy by calling them libertines!"

"Oh, thou heretic! You offspring of Arias! Accursed mouth of Apollinarius that you are! "

At this the hermit who had been bewailing his lapse from virtue fell upon his comrade and began beating him with all his might. When the outburst was over, they walked silently to their caves.

All night long the repentant one was wearing himself out with grief, filling the desert with his groans and cries, tearing his hair, throwing himself on the ground and dashing his head against it, whilst the other was quietly and happily singing his psalms.

Next morning the repentant hermit was struck by a sudden thought: "By my many years of self–denial I had been granted a special blessing of the Holy Spirit which had already begun to reveal itself in miracles and apparitions. Now, if *after this* I gave myself up to the abominations of the flesh, I must have committed a sin against the Holy Spirit, which, according to the word of God, is for all eternity unpardonable. I cast a pearl, pure as heaven, before the swine of my reason—those devils —and they have crushed it to powder. Now they will most certainly turn on me and tear me to pieces. If, however, I am irrevocably doomed, what can I do here in the desert?"

And so he went to Alexandria and gave himself up to a wanton life. It so happened that soon he badly wanted money, and, in company with other dissolute fellows like himself, he murdered and robbed a wealthy merchant. The crime was discovered; he was tried by the city court and sentenced to death. He died an unrepentant sinner.

Meanwhile, his old friend , continuing his life of devotion, attained to the highest degree of saintliness, and became famous for his great miracles, so that by the virtue of his mere word, women who had had no children for many years gave birth to men–children. When finally the day of his death arrived, his decrepit and withered body suddenly became resplendent with the beauty of youth. A wondrous light surrounded it; from it proceeded the perfume of sweet spices.

After his death a monastery was built up over his relics, and his name passed from the Alexandrian Church to the Byzantine, and so to the church calendars of Kiev and Moscow. "The lesson of this story," said Varsanophius, "is that all sins are harmless except despondency. The two men committed every iniquity conjointly, but only one of them perished, namely, he who desponded."

GENERAL.— You see, even monks have to be cheerful; whereas nowadays some would like to see soldiers bemoan their sins.

MR. Z.—It seems we have drifted from the question of politeness, but have returned to our principal subject.

LADY.—And here comes the Prince. How are you? In your absence we have been talking about politeness.

PRINCE.—Please excuse me, I could not get away earlier. I received a lot of papers and printed matter from our people. I will show them to you later on.

LADY.—And I will afterwards tell you a holy anecdote, which entertained us in your absence. It was about two monks. But now it is the turn of our Monte Carloist to speak. Now let us hear from you what you have to say about war after our discussion of yesterday.

POLITICIAN.—From yesterday's conversation I remember the reference to Vladimir Monomakh, and the General's military story. Let this be the starting point for the further discussion of the question. It is impossible to deny that Vladimir Monomakh did well when he defeated the Polovtsi, and that the General did his duty when he destroyed the Bashi–Bazouks.

LADY.—That means that you agree.

POLITICIAN.—I agree with what I have had the honor of telling you, namely, that Monomakh and the General acted in the way they were bound to do in *the given situation;* but how are we to appreciate that situation, or to justify the perpetuation of war and militarism?

PRINCE. —That is just what I was about to say.

LADY. Then you agree with the Prince now, don't you?

POLITICIAN. If you will allow me to explain my view of the subject, you will see yourself with whom and with what I do agree. My view is only a logical conclusion drawn from actual life and the facts of history. How can one argue against the historical importance of war when it is the main, if not the only, instrument by which the State has been created and gradually consolidated? Show me a single State which was founded and made secure otherwise than by war.

LADY.— What about the United States?

POLITICIAN. I thank you for an excellent example. I am, however, speaking of the creation of a *State*. The United States, as a European *colony*, was, of course, founded not by war but by exploration, just as all other colonies were. But the moment this colony wished to become a State, it had to earn its political independence by means of a long war.

PRINCE.—Because a State is created by war, which certainly cannot be denied, you evidently conclude that war is important, while I conclude that it proves the unimportance of the State. I mean, of course, for people who have refused to bow down to brute force.

POLITICIAN. —And why do you speak of worshipping brute force? Try to organize a sound community of human beings without Government control, then only can you discuss the non–importance of Governments. Until then, the State and all that you and I owe it, remains an established fact, while your attacks are empty words. Therefore, I repeat: the great historical meaning of war, as the principal condition in the foundation of a State, is beside the question.

But I ask: Must we not consider the great business of forming an Empire as already accomplished in substance? Details can, of course, be arranged even without such heroic measures as war. In ancient times and in the Middle Ages, when the European world of culture was but an island in the middle of an ocean of barbarism, military organization was necessary for self–preservation. People had to be always in readiness to drive away wild hordes, which came from unknown regions to crush dawning civilization.

And now only the non–European elements should be termed islands, while European culture has become the ocean which surrounds them. Our men of science, our adventurers and missionaries have scoured the whole terrestrial globe and have discovered no serious danger to our civilized world. Savages are being successfully exterminated, or are dying out; whilst militant barbarians, like the Turks and Japanese, are being civilized and losing their liking for warfare. In the meanwhile, the process of uniting all the European nations in the common bond of civilized life . . .

LADY (*in a whisper*).—Monte Carlo.

POLITICIAN. . . . In the common bond of civilized life has grown to such an extent that war amongst these nations would really be something in the nature of fratricide, which could not be excused on any grounds now that peaceful settlement of international disputes has become possible. It would be as fantastic in our time to solve such disputes by war as it would be to travel from St. Petersburg to Marseilles in a sailing boat or in a coach driven by a "troika."

I quite agree, of course, that "A lonely sail is looming white in the blue mist of the sea" or "See the troika flitting wild"[1] sounds vastly more poetic than the screeching of railway engines or cries of *"En voiture, messieurs!"* In the same way I am prepared to admit the aesthetic superiority of the "bristling steel of lances" and of "with swinging step in shining array the army is marching along" over the portfolios of diplomats and the cloth–covered tables of peaceful Congresses.

But the serious attitude towards this vital question must, obviously, be entirely independent of the aesthetic appreciation of the beauty which belongs not to real war (this, I can assure you, has very little of the beautiful), but to its reflection in the imagination of the poet and artist. Well, then, once it has been understood by everybody that war, however interesting for poetry and painters (these, of course, could be well satisfied with past wars), is useless now, for it is a costly and risky means of achieving ends which can be achieved at much less cost and in a more certain way by other methods, *it follows then that the military period of history is over.*

I am speaking, of course, *en grand.* The immediate disarmament of nations is out of the question. But I firmly believe that neither ourselves nor our sons will ever see a great war—a real European war—and that our grandsons will learn only of little wars —somewhere in Asia or Africa—and of those from historical works.

My reply concerning Vladimir Monomakh is as follows: When it became necessary to protect the future of the newly–born Russian State from the inroads of Polovtsi, Tartars, etc., war was a most necessary and important enterprise. The same may, to a certain extent, be said about the epoch of Peter the Great, when it was necessary to guarantee the future of Russia as a *European* power. But after that its importance has been becoming ever more disputable, and at the present day, as I have already said, the military period of history is over in Russia, just as it is everywhere else.

And what I have said about our country can be applied, of course, *mutatis mutandis,* to the other European countries. In every one of them war was, in days gone by, the main and inevitable means of defending and strengthening the existence of the State and the nation, and has everywhere lost its *raison d'être* when once this object has been attained.

I may add that I am astonished at the way some modern philosophers discuss the *meaning of war* with reference to the times. Has war any meaning? *C'est selon.* Yesterday it probably had everywhere a rational basis; today it has a rational basis only somewhere in Africa and Middle Asia, where there are still savages. Tomorrow it will be justified nowhere. It is remarkable that with the loss of its rational basis war is, though slowly, losing its glamour. This can be seen even in a nation so backward in the mass as our own.

Judge yourself: the other day the General triumphantly pointed out the fact that all our saints are either monks or soldiers. But I ask you: to what special historical epoch does all this military holiness or holy militarism belong? Does it not form part of that period when war was *in reality* the most necessary, salutary, and, if you will, most holy enterprise? Our saint–warriors were all princes of the Kiev and Mongolian periods, but I fail to recollect any lieutenant–general or other generals amongst them.

Now, what is the meaning of it all? Take two eminent warriors with equal claims to saintship: the one is considered a saint and the other is not. Why, may I ask, is Alexander Nevsky, who beat the Livonians and the Swedes in the thirteenth century, a saint, and why is Alexander Suvorov, who beat the Turks and the French in the eighteenth century, not a saint? Suvorov could not be reproached with anything incompatible with holiness. He was sincerely pious, sang in choirs, read out the Bible from the lectern, led an irreproachable life, was not even any woman's lover, whilst his eccentricities make no obstacle to, but rather supply, a further argument for his being canonized.

The sole difference is that Alexander the Nevsky fought for the national and political future of his country, which, half battered down in the East, could scarcely survive another battering in the West. The intuitive sense of the people grasped the vital importance of the position, and gave the Prince the highest reward they could possibly bestow upon him by canonizing him. Whereas the achievements of Suvorov, though greatly superior in the military sense, particularly his Hannibalian passage of the Alps, did not respond to any pressing need; he was not obliged to save Russia, and so, you see, he has for ever remained merely a military celebrity.

LADY.—But the leaders of the army who fought Napoleon in the year 1812 were not canonized, although they did save Russia.

POLITICIAN. Oh, well, "saving Russia from Napoleon"—that is merely patriotic rhetoric. Napoleon wouldn't have swallowed us up, nor was he *going* to. The fact that we finally got the upper hand certainly revealed our power as a nation and a State, and helped to awaken our national consciousness. But I can never admit that the war of 1812 was caused by any pressing necessity. We could very well have come to terms with Napoleon. But, naturally enough, we could not oppose him without taking some risks, and though the risks proved lucky for us, and the war was brought to an end in a way that greatly flattered our national self-esteem, yet its subsequent effects could hardly be regarded as really useful.

If I see two athletes suddenly without any conceivable reason falling upon each other and one worsting the other, both suffering no harm to their health, I would perhaps say of the victor, "He is a good sport!" but the need of just this particular form of sportsmanship and of no other would remain for me very obscure. The glory of 1812, the national virtues revealed at that time, remain with us, whatever the causes of the war may have been.

"The holy event of 1812
Was still alive in people's eyes."

A poet calls it a "holy event." That is all very fine as far as poetry goes, but I look at the outcome of this "event" and behold the Archimandrite Photius, Magnitzky and Arakcheev on the one hand, and on the other the conspiracy of the Decembrists—i.e., thirty years of the regime of belated militarism which brought about the defeat at Sevastopol.

LADY.—And Pushkin?

POLITICIAN.—Pushkin? . . . Why Pushkin?

LADY.—I read the other day in the newspapers that the national poetry of Pushkin was created by the military glory of the year 1812.

MR. Z.—Not without the special participation of the artillery, as is apparent from the poet's name.[15]

POLITICIAN. Yes; perhaps that is really how it is. To continue my argument, however. As years roll on the uselessness of our wars becomes ever clearer and clearer. The Crimean War is regarded in Russia as very important, as it is generally believed that the liberation of serfs and all the other reforms of Alexander II. were due to its failure. Even supposing this was so, the beneficial effects of an *unsuccessful* war, and only because it was unsuccessful, cannot, of course, serve as an apology for war in general.

If I, without any satisfactory reason, try jumping off the balcony and put my arm out of joint, and later on this dislocation prevents me from signing a ruinous promissory note, I shall be glad afterwards that it had

---

[15] *Pushka* in Russian is a gun.

happened like that; but I will not say that it is generally recommended to jump off a balcony and not to walk down by the stairs. You will agree that when the head is not hurt there is no need for hurting the arm in order to escape signing ruinous agreements; one and the same good sense will save a man both from foolish leaps from a balcony and from foolish signatures.

I believe that even if there were no Crimean War the reforms of Alexander II. would most probably have been carried out, and perhaps in a more secure and far-reaching way. But I am not going to prove this now; we must see that we do not depart from our subject. At any rate, political acts cannot be rated at their indirect and unforeseen consequences; and as to the Crimean War, that is, its commencement brought about by the advance of our army to the Danube in 1853, it had no reasonable justification.

I cannot call sensible the policy which one day saves Turkey from the smashing defeat inflicted on Mehmet Ali by the Pasha of Egypt, thus hindering the division of the Moslem world round two canters, Istanbul and Cairo, which, it seems, would not have done us much harm; and which next day tries to destroy this same redeemed and reinforced Turkey, with the risk of running against the whole of the European coalition. This is not policy, but a sort of Quixotism. The same name I will apply also—I hope the General will pardon me this—to our last Turkish war.

LADY.—And how about the Bashi–Bazouks of Armenia, whom the General destroyed with your full approbation.

POLITICIAN.—I crave pardon. I maintain that, at the present time, war has become *useless,* and the General's recent story is the best illustration of this truth. I quite understand that anybody whose military duty made him an active participant in the war, and who happened to come across irregular Turkish troops inflicting terrible barbarities upon the peaceful population, I say that that man, that every man *(looking at the Prince)* free from preconceived "absolute principles," was obliged by sentiment and by duty alike to exterminate those Bashi–Bazouks without mercy, as the General did, and not to worry about their moral regeneration, as the Prince suggests.

But I beg leave to ask, firstly, who was the real cause of all these atrocities, and, secondly, what has been accomplished by armed intervention? To the first question I can answer in all honor only by pointing to that bad militant policy which irritated the Turks by inflaming the passions and supporting the pretensions of the Christian populations. It was only when Bulgaria began to swarm with revolutionary committees and the Turks became alarmed at possible interference on the part of the European Powers, which would have led the State to inevitable ruin, that the Turks began to slaughter the Bulgarians. The same thing also happened in Armenia.

As regards the second question, what was achieved by intervention? The answer is given by the latest events and is so obvious that everyone can see it. In 1877 our General destroys several thousand Bashi–Bazouks, saving *perhaps* thereby several hundred Armenians. In 1895, in the same locality, similar Bashi–Bazouks murder not hundreds but thousands of the inhabitants. If we are to credit various correspondents (although I do not advise you to believe them), nearly half a million of men were cut to pieces. Well, this may be a fable. However, in any case the Armenian murders were on a considerably greater scale than the Bulgarian atrocities. And these are the beneficent results of our patriotic and philanthropic wars.

GENERAL.—Who can understand this? Here bad politics are to blame and there a patriotic war. One might suppose that Gorchakov and Hiers were soldiers, or that Disraeli and Bismarck were Russian patriots and philanthropists!

POLITICIAN.—Is it possible that my statements are not clear? I have in view a definite connection, not abstract or ideal, but an entirely real, pragmatic connection between the war of 1877, which was itself a result of our bad politics, and of the recent atrocities in Armenia. You may perhaps be aware, or, if not, it may be useful for you to know, what happened after 1878.

Turkey saw from the treaty of San Stefano what awaited her in the future in Europe and decided to guarantee its existence at all events in Asia. First of all, Turkey made sure of England's support at the Berlin Congress; but to be on the safe side, the Turkish Government set about organizing and strengthening its regular army in Armenia, *i.e.,* increasing the number of those "devils" with whom the General had to deal.

This proved to be a good move, because some fifteen years after Disraeli had guaranteed to Turkey the possession of its Asiatic dominions[16] in exchange for the cession of Cyprus, circumstances changed. English policy became anti–Turkish and pro–Armenian; English agitators appeared in Armenia, just as formerly Slavophile agitators had penetrated into Bulgaria. It was then that those "devils," as the General calls them, became "the men of the hour," and with the most

---

[16] On the understanding that reforms should be introduced in Armenia, which Turkey did not do.

polished manners helped themselves to the largest portion of Christian meat which had ever reached their teeth.

GENERAL.— It is disgusting to listen to! And why should the war be blamed for this? Fear God, my friend. If in 1878 statesmen had accomplished their work as satisfactorily as the soldiers did theirs, there would have been no question of strengthening and organizing Turkish irregular troops in Armenia, and consequently no atrocities would have been perpetrated.

POLITICIAN.—That means, you suggest, the final destruction of the Turkish Empire?

GENERAL. Emphatically I do. I am sincerely fond of the Turks, and have much esteem for them. They are a fine people, especially when compared with all these mongrel Ethiopians. Yet I verily believe that it is well–nigh time for us to put an end to this Turkish Empire.

POLITICIAN. I should have nothing to say against this, if those Ethiopians of yours would be able to establish in its place some sort of Ethiopian Empire of their own. But up to the present they can only fight each other, and a Turkish Government is as much necessary for them as the presence of Turkish troops is necessary in Jerusalem for preserving the peace and well–being of the various Christian sects there.

LADY.—I quite expected that you were prepared to give Our Lord's Sepulchre to the Turks forever.

POLITICIAN. And you, of course, think that this would be owing to my being godless or callous, don't you? As a matter of fact, however, my wish to see the Turks in Jerusalem is the reflection of a faint but inextinguishable spark of religious sentiment which I still preserve from my childhood. I know positively that the moment the Turkish soldiers are withdrawn from the streets of Jerusalem all the Christians in the city will massacre each other, after having destroyed all the Christian shrines. If you doubt my impressions and conclusions, just ask any pilgrims whom you may trust, or, what is even better, go and see for yourself.

LADY.—Go to Jerusalem? Certainly not! What more could I see by going there myself? No, I am afraid!

POLITICIAN. Well, that only bears out my statement.

LADY.—How strange. You disagree with the General, but both of you praise the Turks.

POLITICIAN.—The General probably values them as good soldiers, whereas I approve of them as the guardians of peace and order in the East.

LADY. Fine peace and order, indeed, when some tens of thousands of people are suddenly and mercilessly slaughtered. Personally, I would prefer disorder.

POLITICIAN.—As I have already explained, the slaughter was provoked by revolutionary agitation. Why should one demand from the Turks the elevated Christian sentiments of charity and mercy which are not demanded from any other nations, be it even Christians? Please name any country where an armed rising has been quelled without cruel and arbitrary measures.

I am ready to admit that the Turkish Government overdid it, like Ivan IV., when he drowned ten thousand peaceful citizens of Novgorod, or as the commissaries of the French Convention with their *noyades* and *fusillades* or as the English in India when they crushed the mutiny in 1857. All the same, there is no doubt, if the various coreligionaries and Ethiopians, as the General terms them, were left to their own devices, there would be more carnage than under Turkish rule.

GENERAL.—But do I suggest to put the Ethiopians in the place of the Turks? The matter is simple: we should take Constantinople and Jerusalem and make them Russian provinces, under military rule, as in Samarkand or Ashabad. The Turks, when they lay down their arms, might be satisfied and indemnified as regards their religion and in other respects.

POLITICIAN. —Well, I trust you are not speaking seriously, otherwise I should have reason to doubt . . . your patriotism. If we had begun the war with similar radical intentions it would probably have again provoked a European conflict. Ultimately your Ethiopians would have joined the hostile coalition in order to obtain their emancipation. They understand very well that under Russian rule they would not be very free to show "their national spirit," as the Bulgarians say.

And the end of it all would be that, instead of destroying the Turkish Empire, we should have a repetition—only on a grander scale—of the Sebastopol *debacle.* No, though we have indulged in bad politics sufficiently often, I am sure that we shall never see such madness as a new war with Turkey. If we do see it, then every Russian patriot must exclaim with despair: *Quern dens vult perdere, Arius dementat.*

LADY. What does that mean?

POLITICIAN. It means: Him whom God would destroy, He first makes mad.

LADY.—Evidently history is not made to your liking. You are probably as much for Austria as for Turkey?

POLITICIAN.—On that question it is needless for me to expatiate, because more competent people—the national leaders of Bohemia—have long ago declared: "If Austria had not existed it would have been necessary to invent her." The recent parliamentary conflicts in Vienna serve as good illustrations of this aphorism, and present a picture in miniature of what would happen in those countries on the disappearance of the Hapsburg dynasty.

LADY.—And what have you to say about the Franco–Russian alliance? Somehow, you appear to be reticent on that score.

POLITICIAN.—Yes, I do not intend now to enter into the details of that delicate question. In general I may say that a *rapprochement* with a progressive and wealthy nation like France is in every case to our interest. Besides, this alliance is an alliance of peace and a precaution— thus, at least, it is considered in high quarters, where it was concluded and is maintained.

MR. Z. As to the benefits of *rapprochement* between two nations for the development of their morals and culture, this is a complicated matter, which to me seems very obscure. But looking at it from the political point of view, don't you think that by joining one of the two hostile camps on the European continent we lose the advantages of our free position as neutral judge or arbiter between them; we lose our impartiality? By joining one side, and thereby balancing the powers of both groups, don't we create the possibility of an armed conflict between them? It is, for instance, clear that France alone could not fight against the Triple Alliance, whereas with the help of Russia she could certainly do so.

POLITICIAN.—What you observe would be perfectly correct if somebody was interested kindling a European war, but nobody desires to do that. At any rate, it is much easier for Russia to prevent France from leaving the path of peace than it is for France to lure Russia to the path of war, undesirable, as a matter of fact, to both of them. The most reassuring thing, however, is the fact that not only are modern nations averse to waging war, but, what is more important, they *begin to forget how to do it.*

Take the latest collision, the Spanish–American war. Well, what kind of a war was that? A doll's comedy, a fight in a Punch and Judy show!

"After a protracted and murderous war the enemy fell back, having had one man killed and two wounded. We had, no losses." Or again: "The whole of the enemy's fleet, after desperate opposition, surrendered unconditionally to our cruiser. '*Money Enough.*' There were no casualties on either side." And there you have the whole war. I am surprised that all seem to be so little surprised at this new character of war—its bloodlessness, so to speak. The metamorphosis has been taking place before our very eyes, as we all can remember the sort of bulletins published in 1870 and in 1877.

GENERAL.—Don't anticipate events, for when two really military nations come into collision you will soon see what *bulletins* will be issued.

POLITICIAN.—I don't think so. It is not long since Spain was a first–class military nation. It strikes me that in humanity, as in the human body, organs which are not wanted become atrophied; military qualities are not wanted, so they begin to disappear. And if they were to reappear, I should be as much astonished as to see a bat with eagle's eyes or men with tails.

LADY. But how is it, then, that you yourself praised the Turkish soldiers?

POLITICIAN.— I praised them as guardians of peace within the State. In this sense the military power or, as it is said, "the mailed fist," *manus* will yet for a long time be necessary for mankind.

The desire and means for carrying on, international wars, the outcome of national *pugnacity,* is disappearing. It degenerates into that bloodless, though not altogether harmless, form which is exemplified in Parliamentary squabbles. Such a state of things will probably continue as long as opposing parties and opinions exist. To control them the *manes militaris* is indispensable, even when wars—international or internecine—are merely an historical reminiscence.

GENERAL. That is to say, you liken the police to the coccyx, which still exists in man, although only the Kiev witches are credited with proper tails! How very witty! But aren't you just a little too ready with your comparison? Your conclusion is that just because some nation or other degenerates, becomes flabby, and can no longer fight, therefore the military virtues are decadent or lost all the world over! It is possible that under the introduction of "legislative measures" and "systems" even the Russian soldier may soften to jelly! Heaven preserve us!

LADY *(turning to the Politician).* You have not explained yet in what manner, war being excepted, such questions as, for instance, the Eastern

Question should be solved. However wicked the Christian nations in the East may be, they do feel a desire to be independent at any cost, and the Turks do for this reason slaughter them. Surely you don't suggest that we should look on with folded arms? Supposing that your criticisms of the past wars are really sound, I shall ask, like the Prince, though in a different sense: "What are we to do now, should massacres begin somewhere again?"

POLITICIAN.—We must collect our wits before these atrocities begin, and instead of our bad policy adopt a good one, be it even German: not provoking the Turks, and not shouting in an inebriated condition that the Cross must be replaced on St. Sophia.

For our mutual interest we should conciliate Turkey in a quiet and friendly manner. It rests with us to convince the Turks that slaughtering the population is not only a bad but a very unprofitable operation.

MR. Z.—In such admonitions, combined with railway concessions and other commercial and industrial enterprises, the Germans will be sure to anticipate us, and to vie with them would be hopeless.[17]

POLITICIAN. But why should we compete? If somebody does hard work for me, I shall be only too glad and thankful. If, however, this makes me cross with him, so that I ask: "Why did he do it and not I?" I am acting in a fashion which would be unworthy of a respectable man. In the same way it would be unworthy of such a nation as Russia to imitate the dog–in–the–manger, which lying on the hay neither eats nor lets others eat. If others, using their own means, can do more quickly and in a better way the good thing which we also desire, then so much the more profitable is it for us.

I ask you: were not all our wars with Turkey during the nineteenth century waged only for the sake of safeguarding the human rights of the Turkish Christians? Now, what if the Germans achieve the same object in a sure, though peaceful, way by *civilizing* Turkey? It is clear that had they been as firmly established in Asia Minor in 1895 as the English are in Egypt, you may take my word for it we should not have to discuss Armenian massacres any longer.

LADY.—So you also want to put an end to Turkey, but you somehow desire that it should be Germany who should devour her?

---

[17] These words, written by me in October, 1899, were confirmed a month later by the German–Turkish convention concerning matters in Asia Minor and the Bagdad railway.

POLITICIAN.—I admire the wisdom of German policy, for the very reason that it does not want to devour indigestible objects. Germany's policy is more artful: to introduce Turkey into the concert of civilized nations and to assist the Turks to educate themselves. This *modus operandi* would enable them to govern justly and humanely those nationalities which, in consequence of their mutual antagonism, cannot manage their own affairs in a peaceful manner.

LADY.—You are quite a story teller! Is it possible to put a Christian nation under Turkish rule for all time? I admire the Turks in many respects; but all the same, they are barbarians, and their last word will always be brute force. European culture will only make them worse.

POLITICIAN. Exactly the same could be said about Russia at the time of Peter the Great, and even at a much later period. We remember "Turkish barbarities," but how long is it since in Russia, and in other countries as well, that "Turkish barbarities" became unknown? "The poor unhappy Christians groaning under the Moslem yoke!" And what about those who groaned under the yoke of our wicked landlords—were they Christians or pagans? Or what about the soldiers who groaned under the punishment of the rod? However, the only just and reasonable answer to these groans of the Russian peasants was the abolition of serfdom and of the rod, and not the destruction of the Russian Empire.

Why, therefore, should the reply to Bulgarian and Armenian atrocities be necessarily the destruction of Turkey, where these groans are heard but may be prevented?

LADY.—It is not the same thing when disorders take place in Christian countries, where they can easily be set right, as when a Christian nation is oppressed by non–Christians.

As to your distinction between "Christians" and "non–Christians," you will do well to remember that for the victims of barbarities this question is lacking in interest. If anybody strips off my skin, I shall surely not ask him: "What is your religion, sir? "Neither shall I be at all consoled if I find out that the people torturing me are not only extremely unpleasant and disturbing to me, but on the top of this, being Christians themselves, are exceedingly abhorrent to their own God, who sees His commands openly defied.

Speaking objectively, it cannot be denied that the "Christianity" of Ivan the Terrible, or Saltykova, or Arakcheiev[18] is not in any sense an

---

[18] The Moscow landlady of the middle of the 18th century, Saltykova, and the favourite of Alexander I., General Arakcheiev, have become famous in Russia for the monstrous atrocity with which they treated those under their power. (Translator.)

advantage, but rather so utterly base that it is impossible to meet with its like in other religions. Yesterday the General was describing the dastardly deeds of the savage Kurds, and amongst other things he mentioned their Devil–worship. It is certainly very wicked to roast babies or grown–up people over a slow fire—I am quite prepared to call such acts devilish. It is a well–known fact, however, that Ivan the Terrible was particularly fond of this very roasting of men on a slow fire, and that he even stirred the coals with his staff. but rather a man of keen intellect, and, for the age in which he lived, a man of wide learning, whilst at the same time he was also a theologist firmly attached to orthodoxy. But we need not probe so far into the remote past.

Take the Bulgarian Stamboulov and the Serbian Milan—are they Turks, or are they representatives of the so–called Christian nations? What is, then, this "Christianity" of yours if not an empty title, which carries with it no guarantee for anything?

LADY. One would think it is the Prince expounding his faith. How strange!

POLITICIAN.—When it is a question of a self–evident truth I am not only in sympathy with our highly–respected Prince but even with Balaam's ass.

MR. Z.—Your Excellency in kindly taking a leading part in our conversation did not, I presume, entertain the intention of discussing Christianity or Biblical animals. Even at the present moment there still sounds in my ear your heart's cry of yesterday: "Only as little religion as possible! For God's sake, as little religion as you can help!" That being so, would you kindly return to the subject and explain one little thing that is puzzling me?

On the other hand, as you also admitted on quite reasonable grounds, that we must not destroy the Turkish Empire, but civilize it. You also stated that Germany is much more fitted to civilize the Turks than we are. Now, if both these statements are correct, will you be good enough to tell me what in your opinion there is left for Russia as an object for a special and solely Russian policy in the Eastern question?

POLITICIAN.—In what? I should have thought it was clear, we have no function. Under the title of a special function of Russian policy you, of course, understand that Russia should herself solve the problem, in opposition to the aspirations of all the other European nations. But I may tell you that such a policy has never existed. We have deviated, for instance, in the fifties and the seventies, from this plan, but those sad deviations are precisely what I term bad politics, and have instantly brought their own reward in the shape of reverses of greater or smaller significance.

Speaking in general, Russian policy in the Eastern Question cannot be considered independent or isolated. Her problem, from the sixteenth and even to the end of the eighteenth century, consisted in protecting the civilized world, conjointly with Poland and Austria, from the threatened Turkish invasion. This defensive measure (even without a formal alliance) rendered it necessary to act together with the Poles, the Austrians and the Venetian Republic. It was a common policy and not not an independent one. In the nineteenth century, and much more so in the twentieth century, its co-operative character must remain the same as before, though naturally its objects and means have of necessity changed.

The problem now is not to defend Europe from Turkish barbarism, but to make the Turks themselves more European. For the old object the means required were military; for that of the present day they must be peaceful. Both in the first case as well as in the second the object itself remains constant: as formerly the European nations were bound in solidarity by the interests of military defense, so today they are bound in solidarity by the interests of spreading civilization.

GENERAL.—However, the former military solidarity in Europe did not prevent Richelieu and Louis XIV from entering into alliances with Turkey against the Hapsburgs.

POLITICIAN.—It was a bad Bourbon policy, which, combined with their foolish internal politics, duly received its just reward from history.

LADY. You call it history: I believe it used to be termed *regicide*.

MR. Z.—But that exactly means *wicked* history.

POLITICIAN *(turning to the Lady)*.—The fact is that no political mistake remains unpunished.

Those inclined to look that way, may see in this something mystical. So far as I am concerned, I find as little of it in this case as I should find were I, in my present age and position, to start drinking champagne, glass after glass, as if I were a young man, instead of satisfying myself with a milk diet. I should undoubtedly become ill, and were I too persistent in my *ancien regime* it would kill me as it did the Bourbons.

LADY.—But you will agree that your *milk* diet becomes as wearisome as the Bourbons.

POLITICIAN *(offended).—If* I were not interrupted, I would long ago have exhausted the question and made room for a more entertaining speaker.

LADY.—Well, well, don't be offended. I was only joking. On the contrary, in my opinion you are very witty—for your age and position.

POLITICIAN.—I was saying, we are now in agreement with the rest of Europe as regards the *cultural* transformation of Turkey, and that we have not, and need not have, any special independent policy of our own. It must, however, be admitted that on account of our comparative backwardness in social development, in industry and trade, the share of Russia in this common cause of civilizing the Turkish Empire cannot at present be very great.

The foremost importance which our country had as a military State cannot, of course, be retained by us now. Predominance is not acquired for nothing; it must be earned. We earned our military importance not by mere bluff, but by actual wars and victories. In the same way, our importance in the work of civilization must be earned by actual labor and successes in peaceful callings.

As the Turks had to fall back before our military victories, they will now retire before those who prove themselves to be strongest in the sphere of peaceful progress. What is there left for us to do, in that case? You will hardly meet anywhere now with that blatant insanity which believes that the mere ideal of the imaginary raising of the cross on St. Sophia is a more powerful force in itself than is the actual superiority of the Germans.

GENERAL—The point is that the Cross should not be imaginary.

POLITICIAN.—Then what is to materialize the Cross? So long as you have not found the means to do so, the only thing demanded by our national ambition —within the reasonable limits, of course, in which this feeling could be recognized at all—is to double our efforts so that we could as quickly as possible come into line with other nations in what we lag behind them, and by doing so, gain the time and effort wasted on various Slav committees and similar pernicious nonsense.

Besides, if we are as yet powerless in Turkey, we are already capable of playing a leading part in civilizing Central Asia, and particularly the Far East, whither, it appears, the history of the world is transferring its center of gravity. Owing to her geographical situation, and other advantageous conditions, Russia can do more there than any other nation, except, of course, England.

It follows, then, that the object of our policy in this respect must be to secure a permanent and amiable understanding with England, so that our cooperation with her in the work of civilization may never change into a senseless hostility and unworthy rivalry.

MR. Z.—Unfortunately similar transformations among men as well as in nations are only brought about, as if it were a part of their destiny.

POLITICIAN.—Yes, that is how it happens. However, neither in the life of men nor of nations do I know a single example where enmity and envy between peoples engaged in the same work made any one stronger, richer or happier. This universal experience, to which not a single exception could be found, is being made use of by clever people. And I believe that such a clever nation as Russia will not fail to make use of it either. To quarrel with the English in the Far East—why, this would be the most utter madness, not to speak of the indecency of indulging in domestic quarrels before strangers. Or do you perhaps think that we are more closely related to the yellow–faced Chinese than to the compatriots of Shakespeare and Byron?

MR. Z.—That is a delicate question.

POLITICIAN.—Let us put it aside for the present and turn to another question. Will you adopt my point of view and admit that at present the policy of Russia can have only two objects? First, the maintenance of European peace, since every European war in the present state of historical development must be a useless and wicked civil war. And second, the exercise of civilizing authority on barbarous nations which are in our sphere of influence.

Both these objects, independently of their intrinsic worth, support and guarantee each other's existence. While working to civilize barbarous countries, which is for the interest of all Europe, we draw more closely the bonds of union between ourselves and other European nations.

The confirmation of European unity, in its turn, strengthens our influence on barbarous nations, as we thus leave them no hope of successful resistance. Don't you think that if the yellow man knew that all Europe were behind Russia, we could do in Asia anything we wish? If, however, he saw that Europe were not behind Russia, but against her, he would not hesitate even to attack our frontiers, and we should have to defend ourselves on two fronts, over a line ten thousand versts long. I do not believe in the "Yellow Peril," because I do not admit the possibility of a European war. But given the latter, we should, of course, have to fear even the Mongolians.

GENERAL.—You consider a European war and an invasion of Mongols improbable, yet I fear that your "solidarity" of the European nations and the advent of universal peace are also improbable. It appears somehow unnatural and improbable. There is good reason for singing in churches on Christmas–day, "Peace on earth and goodwill towards men." That means that there will be peace on earth only when there is goodwill among men. But when will that be? Have you seen it? To tell the truth, the only State in Europe that you and I feel friendly towards is the Principality of Monaco. We are always at peace with that State. But close friendship with the Germans and the English and "solidarity" with them, as you call it, will never be realized.

POLITICIAN.—How do you mean it will never be realized; it is already realized, in the natural order of things. We are in "solidarity" with Europeans for the very simple reason that we are Europeans. Since the eighteenth century it has been a *fait accompli,* and neither the total lack of culture amongst the Russian masses nor the wild dreams of the Slavophiles can change it.

GENERAL.—But is there solidarity among themselves, for instance between Germans, French and English? It is rumored that even the Swedes and Norwegians have lost their solidarity.

POLITICIAN.—The argument rests on a false basis, for the historical situation has been lost sight of. Did solidarity exist between Moscow and Novgorod in the time of Ivan III and Ivan IV? Why should you then not admit the existence of the present solidarity of the provinces of Moscow and Novgorod in the common interests of the State?

GENERAL.—All I say is, delay proclaiming yourselves Europeans until the European nations form a family, welded together as are the component parts of the Russian Empire. Are we to break up our own solidarity and join the Europeans, who are at daggers drawn among themselves?

POLITICIAN.—At daggers drawn is a strong expression. You may rest in hope. Not only Sweden and Norway, but neither Germany nor France will break up; they will foresee and prevent rupture. The small group of Russian adventurers who back France against Germany ought to be shut up in a fortress, to develop there their patriotism and to preach war against Germany.

LADY. It would really be a very good thing if it were only possible to put in prison all those who foment strife among the nations. But I think you are mistaken.

POLITICIAN.—Well, of course, I spoke *cum grano salis*. No doubt Europe is not entirely united, but I still stand by my historical analogy.

As it was in Russia in the sixteenth century, so it is now in Europe. Separatism existed, but was then at its last gasp; Imperial unity was no more a dream, but was being molded into a definite form. National antagonism was still extant, especially among the uneducated masses and politicians, but it lacked the power to act. A European war could not be provoked.

As to the goodwill of which you are speaking, General, to tell you the truth I fail to see it, not only amongst different nations, but within any nation itself, or even within single families. If you do meet it occasionally, it does not go farther than the first generation. Well then, what conclusion can be drawn from this? Certainly not that this supplies the reason for intestine wars and fratricide. Similarly, in international relationships. The French and Germans may dislike each other if they wish, provided there is no war. I am convinced that there will be none.

MR. Z. This is very probable. But even regarding Europe as one whole, we cannot conclude from this that we ourselves are Europeans. You know there is an opinion, which has become fairly popular during the last twenty years, that Europe, that is, the combination of all the German–Latin nations, is really a distinct type characterized by political unanimity and by common culture and history; it is further maintained that we, Russians, do not belong to this group, but constitute a separate Greco–Slavonic type.

POLITICIAN.— I have heard about this variety of Slavophilism and have even conversed with its votaries. What I then noticed enabled me to solve this question. The fact of the matter is that not all those gentlemen who cry out against Europe and our European notions can adhere to the views adopted by our Greco–Slavonic Church. They are invariably carried away by the teaching of Confucius, Buddha, Tibet Lamas and all manner of Indo–Mongolian Orientalism. Their estrangement from Europe is as great as their gravitation towards Asia. What does that mean?

Let us admit that they are right as regards Europe, that it is a great delusion. But why are they so fatally carried away by the other extreme—by this Asiatic propaganda? And where have their Greco–Slavonic and Orthodox ideas disappeared? For in them was the pith of the matter. Drive out Nature by the door and it gets in by the window. In this instance Nature has no self–existent Greco–Slavonic, cultural, historical type, but was and is Russia, a great frontier country between Europe and Asia.

Being a borderland, our country is naturally more influenced by the Asiatic element than other European States. Herein lies the imaginary idea of our Slav self–existence. Byzantium herself was original, not through anything of her own, but only because of an admixture of the Asiatic element. Whilst with us, from time immemorial, and particularly since the days of the Mongolian yoke, this element has become a part of our nature, our second soul, so much so that the Germans were able to say about us, although not without a sigh:

" Zwei Seelen wohnen, Ach! in *ihrer* Brust
Die eine will sich von der andern trennen."

It is impossible for us to get rid of this second soul, nor is it desirable; for we owe a great deal to it. In order, however, that we may save ourselves from being torn to pieces in such a conflict, as is suggested by the General, it has been necessary that one soul should establish a decisive supremacy over the other, and it stands to reason that this soul should be the better of the two—that it should develop an intellect which is really the more powerful, the more capable of further progress, and the more highly endowed with spiritual possibilities.

Such supremacy was actually established at the time of Peter the Great. But the ineradicable (though finally overpowered) affinity of our soul with Asia even after that led certain minds into meaningless dreams that some chimerical revision of the historical question would settle it once and for ever. Hence Slavophilism, the theory of an original type of historical culture and all the rest of it. As a matter of fact, we are *irrevocably Europeans,* but with an Asiatic sediment at the bottom of our soul. To me it is clear even grammatically. What is "Russian" in the grammatical sense? An adjective. But what is the noun to which it refers?

LADY.—I suppose the noun *man:* Russian man, Russian people.

POLITICIAN. No, that is too general and indefinite. Red Indians and Eskimos are also men, but I cannot agree in regarding as my noun what is common to me and the Redskins and the Eskimos.

LADY. There are things, you know, which are common to all human beings: love, for instance.

POLITICIAN. Well, that is even more general. How can I regard love as my specific property when I know that all other animals, and even miscreants, have it in their nature?

MR. Z. The question is no doubt very complicated. I am, for example, a man of meek character, and in love would be more at one with a white or blue–grey dove than with the black Moor Othello, though he also is called a man.

GENERAL.—Well, at a certain age every reasonable man is in solidarity with white doves.[19]

LADY. Whatever is this?

GENERAL. This pun is not for you, but only for us with his Excellency.

POLITICIAN.—Let us drop this. *Treve de plaisanteries.* We are not on the stage of the Michael Theater. I wished to say that the correct noun for the adjective *Russian* is *European.* We are Russian Europeans just as there are English, French, or German Europeans. If I feel that I am a European, is it not foolish to try and prove that I am a kind of Slavo–Russ or Greco–Slav? I know that I am a European as surely as I am a Russian.

I can, and perhaps even must, pity and protect every man, as every animal too: "Happy is he who shows mercy even to animals"; but I shall regard myself at one, *of the same family,* not with Zulus or Chinamen, but only with the nations and men who have created and preserved all those treasures of culture which form my spiritual nourishment and afford me supreme happiness. Before everything else it was necessary that these chosen nations should form and consolidate themselves, and should resist the onslaught of the lower elements. For this, war was necessary and war was a holy enterprise.

At present they possess the necessary form and strength, and there is nothing they need fear, except internal strife. Now the time has arrived for peace and the peaceful expansion of European culture over all the world. All must become Europeans. The idea expressed by "European" must be as all–embracing as that expressed by "man," and the idea of the European civilized world identical with that of mankind. In this lies the meaning of history. At first there were only Greek Europeans. They were followed by the Roman ones. Next there arose all kinds of others, first in the West, later in the East; then there came Russian Europeans; later—beyond the ocean—the American Europeans; and now must come Europeans who are Turkish, Persian, Indian, Japanese, and possibly even Chinese.

A European is at present a definite *mental conception* which is extending in every sense. Observe, however, the difference. Every man is

---

[19] "White Doves " is the name of a Russian religious sect accused of immoral tendencies. (Tr.)

like any other man. Therefore, if we accept this abstract idea as our essential, we must admit entire personal equality and value the nation of Newton and Shakespeare no higher than we value certain Redskins. This would be too absurd for words, and subversive of practice.

But if my noun is not a man in general, not that empty space with two feet, but a man as a bearer of culture, that is, a European, then nothing is left to support this absurd universal equality. The idea of a *European,* or what is the same, the idea of *culture,* possesses a measure for defining the relative virtues or values of various races, nations, individuals. A sensible policy cannot but take into account all these variations in value.

If it does not do so, if it, for instance, places on the same level a comparatively civilized Austria and some half–wild tribes of Herzegovina, this sort of thing will at once lead us to those stupid and dangerous adventures for which our last pillars of Slavophilism are still longing. *Il y a Européen et Européen.* Even after the cherished and, I hope, not far–distant hour has struck, when Europe or the civilized world will really coincide in extent with the total population of the world, even then there will remain in the unified and pacified mankind all those natural and historically determined gradations and shades in the values of various cultures which will determine our relations with other nations.

Even in the triumphant and all–embracing kingdom of the higher culture, just as much as in the kingdom of Heaven—one glory is of the sun, another glory of the moon, yet other glories of the stars, for one star differs from another in glory—this is, I believe, how it is said in the Catechism, isn't it? How much more is it necessary to guard ourselves from an all–leveling equality in days when this object, though near, is not yet realized?

At the present time, for instance, the papers have told us of more dissensions between England and the Transvaal—that the Boers are even threatening England with a war.[20] I can already see how all sorts of journalists and politicians in Russia, and most probably all over the Continent, will take up arms against England and will cry themselves hoarse in defense of those poor and oppressed Afrikaaners.

Why, it is the same as if our most esteemed, worthy, well–known and learned Mr. Maartens, having entered a neighboring shop to buy something, was suddenly subjected to a violent attack by a dirty shop–boy shouting: "The shop is mine; you are a stranger here; if you don't clear off I will stifle or kill you!"—what time he is already trying to stifle him.

---

[20] The discussion took place in April, 1898. (Author.)

Of course, one would feel pity for our esteemed Mr. Maartens who fell a victim to such a rascally trick. But if this actually happened, I should certainly feel some moral satisfaction if my esteemed friend, having properly thrashed the rascal, had sent him by way of the police court to a home for young criminals. Instead of this, however, we see various respectable people encouraging him and spurring him on. "Clever boy! Fancy a little chap like that being plucky enough to tackle such a great hulking fellow! Go for him, Tommy; we will back you up when you want it! "How disgusting this is!

Why, these Boer keepers and breeders of cattle have not brains enough to proclaim themselves Dutchmen, with whom they are bound by blood–ties. Holland is a real nation, highly cultured, and with great merits to her credit. But no! They regard themselves as a separate nation; they want to create a country of their own. The damned rascals!"

LADY. In the first place, you need not swear. And in the second, tell me what this Transvaal is like, and what kind of people live in it.

MR. Z. The people living there are a mongrel breed of Europeans and negroes; they are neither white nor black; they are "bur'i" (boers).[21]

LADY. Again a *calembour?*

POLITICIAN. And a very high–grade one!

MR. Z. What are the *boers,* such are also the calembours. Though if you don't care for this color, they have there also an *Orange State.*

POLITICIAN.—Speaking seriously, I may say that these Boers are certainly Europeans, but poor specimens. Separated from their great motherland, they have lost to a great extent their culture; surrounded by natives, they have become wilder and coarser themselves To place them on a par with the English, and wish them to be successful in the struggle with England— *cela n'a pas de nom.*

LADY. Didn't your Europeans sympathize with the Caucasian mountaineers when they fought Russia in defense of their independence? And are not Russians far more civilized than Caucasians?

POLITICIAN. I would not care to enlarge upon the motives of this sympathy of Europe with the Caucasian tribesmen. The only thing I will say is that we must assimilate the general European spirit and not be influenced by the accidental stupidities of this or that brand of European.

---

[21] A play upon words; a pun. In Russian "bur'i" means both boers and brown. (Tr.)

From the bottom of my heart I regret, of course, that England, in order to pacify these conceited barbarians, will apparently be compelled to use such an obsolete and historically condemned weapon as war. But if it proves inevitable owing to the degraded state of mind of these Zulus— I mean to say these Boers, encouraged by the foolish envy of England nursed by the Continent, I shall naturally eagerly wish that the war may end as soon as possible with the complete defeat of these African ruffians, so that nobody ever hears talk of their independence again. Should they prove successful—and owing to the distance of their country from England this is not altogether impossible—it would be a triumph of barbarism over culture, and to me as a Russian, that is, a European, the day when that happened would be a day of deep national mourning.

MR. Z. *(to the General, in a low voice).* Ah, how well statesmen can speak. Altogether like that Frenchman: "Ce sabre d'honneur est le plus beau jour de ma vie."

LADY. No; I can't agree with you. Why should not we sympathize with these Boers? We sympathize with William Tell, for instance, do we not?

POLITICIAN.—Well, if they had created their own poetical legend, inspired a home–bred Jean Jacques Rousseau and produced authors and scientists, we would speak differently of them.

LADY. But all that kind of thing happens afterwards; at first the Swiss themselves were shepherds like the Boers. But take other nations. Were the Americans, when they rose against the English to win independence, in any way distinguished in culture? It is true they were not "bur'i"; they were perhaps a little "red–skinned," and used to strip off each other's scalps—according to Captain Mayne Reid.

And yet even Lafayette sympathized with them, and was right, because now, for instance, in Chicago they have managed not only to unite all the religious bodies, but they have made an exhibition of them into the bargain. Nobody has ever seen such a thing before. Paris also wanted to gather together all its religions for the coming exhibition, but nothing came of it, as you doubtless know.

An *abbé,* called Victor Charbonnel, was also very active about it. He wrote to me several times: a very sympathetic man. But the various religions could not agree. Even the Chief Rabbi declared that "for religion we have the Bible, and an exhibition was out of place." Poor Charbonnel was in such despair that he abjured Christ and announced in the newspapers that he had resigned his living and greatly respected Renan. The end of his career, I am told, was not satisfactory, for he married, or took to drink or did something of the kind.

Next came our Nepliuev, who finally lost faith in all religions. He wrote to me that he only believed in a united mankind. He is an idealist. But how was humanity to be represented at the Paris Exhibition? I think it is all too fantastic. The Americans have, however, arranged matters very cleverly. Ecclesiastics representing all religions joined them.

A Catholic bishop was elected president. He read out the Lord's Prayer in English, while the Buddhist and Chinese idolatrous priests responded very politely: "Oh yes! All right, sir! We wish no one evil, and we only beg one thing, that your missionaries should keep away from us. Your religion is very good for you, but you do not practice it. That is not our fault, but our religions are the best for us." And so everything finished satisfactorily, there was no fighting, but much astonishment. Who knows, perhaps modern Africans will in time be like these same Americans. Who knows?

POLITICIAN. Everything is possible, of course. Even the veriest gutter–snipe way later become a scientist. But before this happens you should for his own benefit give him more than one good flogging.

LADY.—What language! *Decidement vous vous encanaillez?* All this comes from Monte Carlo. *Qui est–ce que vous frequentez la bas? Les familes des croupiers, sans doute?* However, that is your business. I would only beg you to curtail your political wisdom or we shall be late for dinner. It is time to stop.

POLITICIAN.—My wish was to sum up, to wind up and to connect the end with the beginning.

LADY.—You will never finish. I must assist to explain your idea. You meant to say, formerly there was a God and there was war, but now instead of God we have culture and peace. Is that so?

POLITICIAN. Well, I think it is near enough.

LADY. Good! Now what God is I do not know, nor can I explain. But I feel it all the same. As to your culture, I have not even a feeling for it. Will you then explain to me in a few words what it is?

POLITICIAN. What are the elements of culture, what it embraces— you know yourself: it includes all the treasures of human thought and genius which have been created by the chosen spirits of the chosen nations.

LADY. But these "chosen spirits" and their creations differ alarmingly. You have, for instance, Voltaire and Rousseau and Madonna, and Nana, and Alfred De Musset and Bishop Philaret. How can you throw all these into one heap and set up this heap for yourself in place of God?

POLITICIAN.—Yes, I meant to say that we need not trouble about culture in the sense of an historical depositary of treasures. It is created; it exists, and we thank God for it. We might hope that there will be new Shakespeares and Newtons, but that is not in our power and is of no practical interest.

There is, however, another practical or moral side to culture. In private life we call it politeness or courteousness. This may appear unimportant to a superficial observer, but it has an immense and exclusive meaning, because it is the only quality which can be universal and obligatory. One cannot demand exalted virtues or genius, but one can and must insist on politeness from everybody. It is the *minimum* of reasonableness and morality which allows men to live like true human beings.

Certainly, politeness is not the *whole* of culture, just as reading and writing does not exhaust mental development, but politeness is necessary *condition* of every form of cultured conduct, just as knowledge of reading and writing, though not the sum total of education, is a necessary condition to it.

Politeness is cultured conduct, *a l'usage de tout le monde.* And we see that from private relations it extends to all social classes, political and international. We remember how in our childhood people could be rude and unrefined, but now obligatory and even coercive politeness has extended its power, and is reaching all classes and countries.

LADY.—Pray be brief. You are trying to prove that peaceful politics between States is the same thing as politeness between people.

POLITICIAN. You are quite correct. It is evidenced in the very words "politeness" and "politics," which obviously are closely related to each other. A remarkable thing is that no special feelings are necessary for this, no such *goodwill,* as was to no purpose mentioned by the General. If I do not fall upon anybody and do not furiously bite his head, this does not mean that I have any goodwill towards that person.

On the contrary, I may nurse in my soul the most rancorous feelings, but as a cultured man I cannot but feel repulsion at biting anybody, and, what is more important, I understand full well that the result of it will be anything but savory, whilst if I abstain from it and treat this man in a polite manner, I shall lose nothing and gain much.

Similarly, whatever may be the antipathies existing between two nations, if they have reached a certain level of culture they will never come to *voies de fait,* that is, to war, and for the patent reason that, in the first place, the real war—not that portrayed in poetry and pictures, but as actually experienced—with all those corpses, foul wounds, crowds of rough and filthy men, the stoppage of the normal order of life, destruction of useful buildings and institutions, of bridges, railways, telegraphs—that a thing so horrid as this must be positively repulsive to a civilized nation, just as it is repulsive to us to see knocked-out eyes, broken jaws, and bitten-off noses. In the second place, at a certain stage of development, the nation understands how profitable it is to be civil to other nations and how damaging to its own interests it will be if it fights them.

Here you, of course, have a number of gradations: the fist is more cultured than the teeth, the stick is more cultured than the fist, and the symbolical slap in the face is even more cultured still. Similarly, wars also can be conducted in a more or less savage way; the European wars of the nineteenth century more resemble a formal duel between two respectable persons than a fight between two drunken laborers. But even this is only a transitional stage.

Note that even the duel is out of fashion in advanced countries. Whereas backward Russia mourns her two greatest poets who have fallen in a duel; in more civilized France the duel has long ago changed into a bloodless offering to a bad and effete tradition. *"Quand on est most c'est qu'on n'est plus en vie,"* M. De-la-Palliss would say, and I am sure we shall still see with you how duels together with war will be relegated for ever to the archives of history. A compromise cannot last long here.

Real culture requires that every kind of *fighting* between men and nations should be entirely abolished. Anyhow, peaceful politics are the measure and the outward sign of the progress of culture. This is why, however anxious I am to please the worthy General, I still stand by my statement that the literary agitation against war is a welcome and satisfying fact. This agitation not only precedes, but actually expedites the final solution of a problem long since ripened. With all its peculiarities and exaggerations, this campaign acquires importance by its emphasizing in the public consciousness the main line of historical progress.

A peaceful, that is, civil, *i.e.,* universally profitable settlement of all international relations and conflicts—such is the fundamental principle of sound politics for civilized mankind. Ah? *(turning to Mr. Z.)* You want to say something?

MR. Z. Oh, it's nothing. It is only about your recent remark that peaceful politics is the symptom of progress. It reminds me that in Turgunev's *Smoke* some person, speaking just as reasonably, says "Progress is a symptom." Don't you think, then, that peaceful politics becomes a symptom of a symptom?

POLITICIAN. Well, what of it? Of course, everything is relative. But what is your idea after all?

MR. Z.—Merely this, that if peaceful politics are only the shadow of a shadow, is it worth talking so much about all this shadowy progress? Would it not be preferable to tell humanity what Father Varsonovius said to the religious lady: "You are old and weak, and will never be any better."

LADY. Well, it's now too late to talk about this. *(To the Politician.)* But you see what a practical joke this politico–politeness of yours has played on you.

POLITICIAN.—How is that?

LADY. Simply that your visit to Monte Carlo, or *par euphemisme,* to Nice will have to be put off tomorrow!

POLITICIAN.—Why so?

LADY. Because these gentlemen here want to reply to you. And as you have been speaking with such prolixity as to leave no time for their replies, they are entitled to do so tomorrow. And surely, at a time when a company of cultured people is busy refuting your arguments, you would scarcely permit yourself to indulge in more or less forbidden pleasures in the company of uneducated croupiers and their families? That would be the height of rudeness. Where, then, is your "obligatory minimum" of morality?

POLITICIAN.—If such is the case, I can put off my trip to Nice for a day or two, as I am curious to hear what can be said against my axioms.

LADY. That's splendid! Now I think everybody is really very hungry, and but for the culture you preach would have long ago made a dash for the dining–room.

POLITICIAN.—It appears to me that culture and the culinary art are closely united.

LADY. —Oh, dear, another joke!

And thereupon, after exchanging some doubtful witticisms, all hastily followed the lady of the house to the dinner awaiting them..

THE THIRD DISCUSSION
"Audiatur et tertia *pars."*

On this occasion, by mutual consent, we assembled in the garden earlier than usual, so as not to be hurried at the end of the conversation. Consequently all were in a more serious frame of mind than the evening before.

POLITICIAN *(to Mr. Z.)*.—You, I believe, wished to raise an objection to something or to make a remark upon what I said recently?

MR. Z.—Yes; with reference to your definition that a peace policy is a symptom of progress, I remembered at once the words of one of the characters in Turgenyev's "Smoke" that "progress is a symptom." I do not know precisely what Turgenyev's character meant by this, but surely the natural meaning of those words is quite accurate. Progress is, in fact, a symptom.

POLITICIAN. A symptom of what?

MR. Z. "It is a pleasure to talk with clever people."[22] That is just the question to which I have been leading. I believe that progress—a visible and accelerated progress—is always *a symptom of the end.*

POLITICIAN.—I understand that where there is such progress as, for example, in a case of creeping paralysis, that is a symptom of the end. But why should the progress of culture and cultured life always be a symptom of the end?

MR. Z.—Well, it is not so apparent as in the case of paralysis; but it is so all the same.

POLITICIAN.—You are convinced, that is clear enough; but to me it is not even clear what it is of which you are convinced. In the first place, I am encouraged by your praise to put again the simple question, which you thought clever. You say, "a symptom of the end." The end of *what?* I ask.

MR. Z.—The end of that of which we were talking. We were discussing the history of mankind; that historic "process" which certainly has begun to go at an ever-increasing speed, and as I am convinced draws near to its conclusion.

LADY.—*C'est la fin du monde, n'est-ce pas?* The argument is becoming a most extraordinary one!

---

[22] A Russian proverb. (Translator.)

GENERAL.—Well, at last we have reached the most interesting subject.

PRINCE. You will not, of course, forget Anti–Christ either.

MR. Z. Certainly not. He takes the most prominent place in what I have to say.

PRINCE *(to Lady)*. Pardon me, please. I am now exceedingly busy on very urgent matters. I am very anxious to hear the discussion on this most fascinating subject, but, I am sorry to say, I must return home.

GENERAL. Return home? And what about whist?

POLITICIAN. I had a presentiment from the very first day that some villainy or other was being prepared. Where religion is involved, never expect any good. *Tantum religio potuit suadere malorum.*

PRINCE.—There will be no unpleasantness. I will try to come back at nine o'clock, but now I really have no time.

LADY. — Why this sudden urgency? Why did you not think about those important matters before? I do not believe you. You must admit that it is "Anti–Christ" that has suddenly frightened you away.

PRINCE.—I heard so much yesterday about politeness being the thing of first importance that, acting under that suggestion, I decided to tell an untruth for the sake of politeness. Now, I see, that this is very wrong, and I will say frankly that, though I have in fact important business, I am leaving this conversation chiefly because I consider it useless to waste my time in an argument about things which can be of interest only to Papooses and such like.

POLITICIAN. Your very polite sin is now expiated, it seems.

LADY.—Why get angry? If we are stupid, enlighten us. Look at me, I certainly am not angry because you called me a papoose. Why, even Papooses may have correct ideas. God makes infants wise. But if it is so difficult for you to hear about Anti–Christ, we'll agree on this: Your villa is only a few steps from here. You go home to your work now, and towards the end of the discussion come back—after Anti–Christ. . . .

PRINCE.—Very well, I will come back.

(When the Prince had gone the GENERAL remarked, laughing).— The cat knows whose meat she has eaten.[23]

---

[23] A Russian proverb. (Tr.)

LADY. What, you think our Prince is an Anti–Christ?

GENERAL. Well, not personally, not he personally; it will be a long time before he gets as far as that. But he is on the right track, all the same. As it is said in the Gospel of St. John: "You have heard, my little ones, that Anti–Christ is coming, and there are many Anti–Christs now." So, one of these "many . . ."

LADY.— One may find oneself amongst the "many" against one's wish. God will not punish him for that. He simply has been led astray. He knows that he will never do anything remarkable, only walk about in a smart uniform and set himself up as though he had got into the guards from a line regiment. To a great general all this does not matter, but for a small officer it is very flattering.

POLITICIAN. —That is good psychology. All the same, I do not understand why he became angry at the mention of Anti–Christ. Here am I, for instance. I do not believe in anything mystic, yet it does not make me angry, but rather interests me from the human point of view. I know that to many it is a serious matter; that is to say, it gives expression to a certain side of human nature which is somewhat atrophied in me, but it preserves its objective interest for me too.

For example, I am altogether bad at painting and can draw nothing—not even a straight line or a circle—so I do not discuss amongst painters what is well drawn and what badly drawn. But I am interested in questions of painting on educational and aesthetic grounds.

LADY. It is difficult to be offended at such a harmless thing as art. But religion, for instance, you hate with all your heart, and only just now you quoted some Latin curse against it.

POLITICIAN. — A curse! Good gracious! In the words of my favorite poet Lucretius, I merely blamed religion for its bloodstained altars and the cries of the human beings sacrificed upon them. I can hear an echo of this bloodthirstiness in the gloomy–intolerant utterances of the companion who has just left us.

Still, religious ideas *per se* interest me very much—amongst others this idea of the "Anti–Christ." Unfortunately, all I have been able to read on this subject is confined to the book by Renan, and he considers the question only in relation to historical evidence, which in his opinion points indubitably to Nero. But this is not sufficient.

We know that the idea of "Anti–Christ" was held by the Jews long before the time of Nero—and was applied by them to the King Antiochus

Epiphanes. It is still believed in by the Russian "Old–Believers," so there must be some truth in it, after all.

GENERAL. The leisure your Excellency enjoys affords you every opportunity for the discussion of such high matters. But our poor Prince employs so much of his time in preaching evangelical morals that he is naturally prevented from pondering on Christ or Anti–Christ: even for his whist he cannot get more than three hours a day.

LADY. You are very hard on him, General. It is true that all of his crowd seem unnatural, but then they look so miserable, too: you won't find in them any joy, good humor, or placidity. Yet is it not said in the Gospels that Christianity is the joy of the Holy Ghost?

GENERAL. The position is, indeed, very difficult: to be lacking in Christian spirit, and yet to pass themselves off as true Christians.

MR. Z. As Christians *par excellence* without possessing what constitutes the real excellence of Christianity.

GENERAL.—But it seems to me that this sad position is the precise position of Antichrist which for the more wise or enlightened is overburdened with the consciousness that in the long run deceit, of course, will not pay.

MR. Z.—At all events, it is certain that the idea of Antichrist, which according to its Biblical interpretation—both of the Old and New Testaments—is the last act of the historic tragedy, will not be simple unbelief or negation of Christianity, or materialism and such like, but that it will be religious imposture, when with the name of Christ will be associated forces in human nature which are in fact and in essence foreign, and plainly hostile to Christ and His Spirit.

GENERAL.—Naturally so. The Devil would not be what he is if he were to play in the open!

POLITICIAN.—I fear, then, lest all Christians should turn out to be impostors and therefore according to you, Antichrists. The only possible exceptions would be the unconscious masses of the people, as far as such still exist in the Christian world, together with a certain number of individual cranks, like you, Sir. But in any case, one ought to regard as Antichrists those people—both here in France and with us—who particularly make a fuss about Christianity, who make of it their special occupation, and make it the profession of a sort of monopoly or privilege of their own.

Such people at the present time belong to one of two classes which are equally foreign, I hope, to the spirit of Christ. They are either mad slaughterers, who are ready at once to restore the Inquisition and to arrange religious massacres, like those pious abbots and "brave" "Catholic" officers who recently gave vent to their feelings on the occasion of celebrating some detected swindler.[24]

Or they may be the new ascetics and celibates who have discovered virtue and conscience as some new America, whilst losing at the same time their inner truthfulness and common sense. The first cause in one a moral repulsion. The second make one yawn for very boredom.

GENERAL. This is quite true. Even in the past, Christianity was unintelligible to some and hateful to others. But it remained to our time to make it either repulsive or so dull that it bores men to death. I can imagine how the 'Devil rubbed his hands and laughed until his stomach ached when he learned of this success. Good gracious me!

LADY. Well, is this Anti–Christ as you understand him?

MR. Z. Oh, no! Some signs indicating his nature are given here, but he himself is still to come.

LADY. Then will you explain in the simplest way possible what the matter really is?

MR. Z.—Well, I cannot guarantee simplicity. It is difficult to assume true simplicity whenever you wish. But a sham, artificial, false simplicity—nothing can be worse than that. There is an old saying which was often repeated by a friend of mine, now dead: *"Great simplicity is misleading."*

LADY. This is not so simple either.

GENERAL. I believe it is the same as the popular proverb: "Some simplicities are worse than robbery."

MR. Z. You've guessed it!

LADY. Now I understand it too.

---

[24] The Politician obviously refers here to the public subscription opened in commemoration of the " suicide " Henry, in which one French officer stated that he subscribes in the hope of seeing a new St. Bartholomew massacre; another officer wrote that he was looking forward to an early execution of all Protestants, Freemasons, and Jews, whilst an abbé confessed that he lived by anticipation of that glorious time when the skin stripped off the Huguenots, the Masons, and the Jews will be used for making cheap carpets, and when he will, as a good Christian, always tread such a carpet with his feet. These statements, amongst tens of thousands of others in a similar vein, were published in the paper, La Libre Parole. (Author.)

MR. Z. It is a pity, though, that one cannot explain all about Anti-Christ by proverbs.

LADY. Then explain as best you can.

MR. Z.— Very well then. First of all, tell me, do you recognize the existence and power of evil in the world?

LADY. —I would prefer not to recognize it, but one can hardly help doing so. Death alone would make one believe it: for death is an evil one cannot escape. I verily believe that "the last enemy to be destroyed will be death"—but before it is destroyed, it is clear that evil is not only strong in itself but even much stronger than good.

MR. Z. (to the General).— And what is your opinion?

GENERAL. I have never shut my eyes before bullets and shells, and shall certainly not do so when faced with subtle questions. Certainly, evil is as real as good. There is God, but there is the Devil also—of course, so long as God tolerates him.

POLITICIAN. As for myself, I shall abstain from a definite answer for a time. My view does not go deeply to the root of the matter, and that side of it which is clear to me I explained as best I could yesterday. But I am interested to know what other people think of it. I can understand perfectly well the Prince's mode of thought. In other words, I understand that there is no real thought in his case at all, but only a naked pretension *qui n'a ni rime ni raison.*

The positive religious view, however, is much more intelligent and more interesting. Only up to the present all my acquaintance with it was confined to its official form, which affords me very little satisfaction indeed. I should be very pleased to hear, instead of the vapourings of mealy-mouthed parsons, the natural human word.

MR. Z. Of all the stars that rise on the mental horizon of a man who carefully reads our Sacred Books, I think there is none so clear, illuminating, and startling as that shining in the phrase of the Gospel, "Thinkest thou that I come to bring peace on Earth? I come not to bring peace, but a sword." He came to bring *truth* to the earth, and truth, like good, before everything else *divides.*

LADY. This needs to be explained. If you are right, why is it that Christ is called the Prince of Peace, and why did He say that peacemakers will be called the children of God?

MR. Z.—And are you really wishing me to obtain that higher status by reconciling contradictory texts?

LADY.—Precisely.

MR. Z.—Well, notice that the only way of reconciling them is by making a distinction between good or true peace and the peace which is bad or false. This distinction is plainly pointed out by Him who brought a true peace and a good enmity: "My peace I leave with you, My peace I give unto you: Not as the world giveth, Give I unto you."

There is therefore the good peace—the peace of Christ, resting on the *division* which Christ came to bring to the world, namely, the division between good and evil, between truth and untruth. There is also the bad peace— founded on a confusion or the peace of the world which endeavors to blend or to unite together externally elements which internally are at war with one another.

LADY.—How do you explain the difference between good and bad peace?

MR. Z. In very much the same way as the General did when, the other day, he remarked in a jocular way that one may have a good peace like that, for instance, concluded by the treaties of Nishstadt or of Kutchuk–Kainardzh. Beneath this joke lies hidden a serious and significant meaning. In spiritual strife as in political, a good peace is one which is concluded only on obtaining the object of the war.

LADY.—But in the last resort whence arises the war between good and evil? Is it absolutely necessary for them to fight one against the other? And can there be between them a real collision—*corps á corps*? In the ordinary war, when one side becomes the stronger, the opposing side also looks for reinforcements, and the struggle has to be decided by pitched battles, with guns and bayonets.

You will find nothing like this in the struggle between good and evil. In this struggle, when the good side becomes stronger, the bad side immediately weakens, and the struggle never leads on to a real battle. So that all this must be taken only in a metaphorical sense. Thus it is one's duty to foster the growth of good in man. Evil will then diminish as a matter of course.

MR. Z. In other words, you believe that it is enough for kind people to grow still kinder, and that then wicked people would go on losing their malice until finally they become as kind as the others.

LADY. I believe that is so.

MR. Z.—Well, are any occasions known to you when the goodness of a good man made the bad man good or at least less wicked?

LADY. No, candidly I do not. Neither have I seen or heard of such cases. . . . But, pardon me, is not what you have said just now similar to what you were discussing with the Prince the other day? That even Christ, however kind He was, could not convert the souls of Judas and the impenitent thief? You will not forget that the Prince has still to answer this, will you?

MR. Z. Well, since I don't believe the Prince to be Anti–Christ, I have little faith in his coming, and still less in his theological presence of mind. However, in order to relieve our discussion from the burden of this unsolved question, I will state the objection which the Prince should make *from his standpoint.* "Why did not Christ regenerate the wicked souls of Judas and Co. by the power of His goodness? "For the simple reason, the answer would run, that it was a dark time, and only a few choice souls reached that degree of moral development which allows of an adequate response to the inner power of truth. And Judas and Co. were too "backward" for that.

Furthermore, Jesus Himself said to His disciples: "Deeds which I do, you will do also, and even *more* than this you *will do.*" It follows that at a higher stage of moral progress in mankind, such as is reached at the present time, the true disciples of Christ are able by the power of their kindness, and by forcibly refusing to resist evil, to perform moral miracles surpassing even those which were possible eighteen centuries ago. . . .

GENERAL. Just a moment! If they are *able* to perform miracles, why don't they? Or have you seen some of these new miracles? Even now, after "eighteen centuries of moral progress in Christian consciousness," our Prince is still unable to enlighten my dark soul. Just as I was a barbarian before I met him, so I remain. I am just what I have always been.

After God and Russia, what I love most is military work in general, and the artillery in particular. And in my lifetime I have met not only our Prince, but other non–resisters as well, and some perhaps even mightier than he.

MR. Z.—Now, why get on to such personal grounds? and what do you want of me? I put before you on behalf of our absent opponent a passage of the Gospel which he had forgotten, and beyond that

> "Whether it reason or unreason seem—
> I do not answer for another's dream."

LADY. Now I think I must defend our poor Prince. If he wanted to be really clever, he would say to the General: "I and those whom you have found to hold my views consider ourselves to be true disciples of Christ, but only in the sense of a general trend of thought and action, and not of having any greater power of doing good. But we are certain that there are, or will shortly be somewhere, Christians more perfect than we are—they may penetrate your stronghold of darkness."

MR. Z.—This answer, of course, would be of practical utility were it not that it made its appeal to unknown instances. But as it is, it is not serious. They, let us 'suppose, say, indeed they must say—we can do nothing either greater than that which Christ did, nor equal to His works nor even less than them, but only something which approximates to them. What in sound logic must be deduced from such an avowal?

GENERAL. —Apparently, only this, that the words of Christ: "Ye shall do what I have done and greater works than these" were said not to these men, but to some other person altogether unlike them.

LADY. Yet it is possible to imagine that some man will carry out Christ's commandment about loving his enemies and forgiving those who do wrong to him. And then he will, with the help of Christ Himself, acquire the power to convert wicked souls into good ones.

MR. Z. Not so long ago an experiment was tried in this direction, and not only did it not realize its object, but it actually proved the very opposite to what you are supposing now. There lived a man whose kindness knew no bounds. He not only forgave every wrong done to him, but for every evil returned deeds of kindness. Now what do you suppose happened? Do you think he stirred the soul of his enemy and regenerated him morally? Alas! he only exasperated the evil spirit of the villain, and died miserably by his hand.

LADY.—What are you talking about? Who is this man? Where and when did he live?

MR. Z.—Not so long ago, and in Petersburg. I thought you knew him. He was the chamberlain Delarue.

LADY.—I have never heard of him, and I thought I could tell off the whole of Petersburg on my fingers.

POLITICIAN.—I, also, do not remember him. But what is the history of this chamberlain?

MR. Z.—It is excellently set forth in an unpublished poem by Count Alexis Tolstoy.

LADY.—Unpublished? Then, of course, it is a mere farce. What has this got to do with serious matters?

MR. Z. I can assure you, madam, that, farcical though it is in its form, it contains a very serious story, and, what is more to the point, one true to life. At any rate, the actual relationship between kindness and wickedness in human life is portrayed in these amusing verses with a much greater skill than I could ever show in my serious prose.

Moreover, I have not the slightest doubt that when the heroes of some world-wide popular novels, skillfully and seriously tilling the psychological mould, have become a mere literary recollection for book-lovers, this farce, which in an exaggerated and wildly caricatured form plumbs the very depth of the moral problem, will retain all its artistic and philosophic truth.

LADY.—Well, I do not believe in your paradoxes. You are afflicted with the spirit of contradiction, and you always defy public opinion on purpose.

MR. Z.—I should probably have "braved" it had it really existed. Still, I am going to tell you the story of court chamberlain Delarue, since you do not know it, and I happen to remember it by heart :

> The wicked robber plunged his dagger
>   In the breast of Delarue ;
> And he, for his part, lifted his hat and said,
>   " Dear Sir, I thank you."
> Then in the left side the robber struck again
>   His dreadful dagger,
> And Delarue said, "What a splendid dagger
>   That is of yours."
> Then also the right side this cruel robber
>   Pierced as before,
> But Delarue with a gentle smile
>   Barely reproved him.
> The miscreant then raised his dagger up
>   And struck him in a hundred places ;
> Said Delarue, "I pray you, Sir,
>   To come to tea at three o'clock tomorrow."
> The wicked man in tears then fell upon the ground
>   And trembled like a leaf.
> But Delarue said, "Oh, oh, dear Sir, get up,
>   The floor is dirty " ;
> But the robber would not be comforted
>   And wept the more.
> Then Delarue said, "How strange is this!
>   I could not have expected it ;
> To weep in such a way for such a little thing
>   Isn't possible!
> I'll let you have a nice estate to farm,
>   The order of Stanislas
> I'll pin upon your breast, friend,

>   For an example.
> A word from me to the authorities procures it—
>   I'm chamberlain.
> My daughter Mary in marriage
>   I will give,
> And a hundred thousand rubles, Sir,
>   My daughter's dowry.
> Meanwhile do take this little portrait of myself
>   In memory.
> I'm sorry it is not framed, but take it so
>   From me."
> The murderer got up, but bitterer than pepper
>   Was his mood ;
> The portrait gift he could forgive,
>   But not the offers.
> He hardly had the Stanlislavsky order
>   Upon his breast
> Than a godless rage possessed him, and his dagger
>   Dipped he in poison,
> And he laid in wait for Delarue
>   And stabbed him once again.
> Down fell Delarue to the ground, being unable
>   To remain in his armchair,
> And the other rushed upstairs and in the entresol
>   Seduced his daughter,
> And then fled to Tambov, where, as Governor,
>   He was by all beloved.
> Afterward he lived in Moscow, a senator
>   By all esteemed.
> Then our House of Lords he joined
>   For a short season.
> What an example was he to us all,
>   And what a lesson!

LADY. Oh, how sweet it is, how sweet! I never anticipated anything so delightful!

POLITICIAN.—Really excellent. "My daughter's dowry"—admirable. "Not the offers!" and "Then fled to Tambov!"—*deux vrais coups de maitre!*

MR. Z. But note how true to life all this is. Delarue is not a specimen of that "purified virtue" which one never meets in nature. He is a real man with all the human weaknesses. He is vain ("I am a chamberlain," he says) and fond of money (he has managed to save ten thousand pounds); whilst his fantastic immunity from the stabs of the villain's dagger is, of course, merely an obvious symbol of his infinitely good humor, invincible, even insensitive to all wrongs—a trait also to be met with in life, though comparatively seldom.

Delarue is not a personification of virtue, but a naturally kindhearted man, in whom kindness overpowered all his bad qualities, driving them to the surface of his soul and revealing them there in the form of inoffensive weaknesses.

The "villain" also is not the conventional essence of vice, but the normal mixture of good and bad qualities. The evil of envy, however, rooted itself in the very depth of his soul and forced out all the good in him to the *epidermis* of the soul, so to speak, where the kindness became a sort of very active but superficial sentimentality.

When Delarue replies to a number of offensive actions with polite words and with an invitation to tea, the villain's sentimentality is greatly moved by these acts of gentleness, and he descends to a climax of repentance. But when later the chamberlain's civility is changed into the sincere sympathy of a deeply good-natured man, who retaliates upon his enemy for the evil done, not with the seeming kindness of nice words and gestures, but by the actual good of practical help

When, I say, Delarue shows interest in the life of his enemy, is willing to share with him his fortune, to secure for him an official post, and even to provide him with family happiness, then this *real* kindness, penetrating into the deeper moral strata of the villain, reveals his inner moral emptiness, and when it reaches the very bottom of his soul it arouses the slumbering crocodile of envy.

It is not the kindness of Delarue that excites the envy of the villain— as you have seen, he can also be kind, and when he cried, pitifully wringing his hands, he doubtless was conscious of this. What did excite his envy was the—for him—unattainable infinite vastness and *simple seriousness* of that kindness :

" Assassins may forgive the gift of a portrait; Not pension and place."

Is it not realistic? Do we not see this in everyday life? One and the same moisture of vivifying rain causes the development of healing powers in some herbs and of poison in others. In the same way, a real act of kindness, after all, only helps to develop good in the good man and evil in the evil one.

If so, how can we—have we even the right to let loose our kind sentiments without choice and distinction? Can we praise the parents for zealously watering from the good can the poisonous flowers growing in their garden, where their children play? I ask you, why was Mary ruined?

GENERAL. With this I fully agree! Had Delarue given a good drubbing to the villain and chucked him out afterwards, the fellow would not have had time for fooling upstairs.

MR. Z. I am prepared to admit that he had the right to sacrifice himself to his kindness. Just as in the past there were martyrs of faith, so in our time I can admit there must be martyrs of kindness. But what, I ask you, should be done with Mary? You know, she is silly and young, and cannot, nor does she wish, to prove anything by her own example. Is it possible, then, not to pity her?

POLITICIAN. I suppose. it is not. But I am even more sorry for the fact that Anti–Christ seems to have fled to Tambov with the villain.

MR. Z. Never mind, your Excellency, we'll catch him right enough! Yesterday you were pleased to point out the meaning of history by reference to the fact that natural mankind, at first consisting of a great number of more or less savage races, alien to each other, partly ignorant of each other, partly actually engaged in mutual hostilities.

That this mankind gradually evolves from within itself its best and most educated part—the civilized or European world, which ever grows and spreads until it embraces all other groups lagging behind in this historical development, and blends them into one peaceful and harmonious international whole. Establishing a permanent international peace—such is your formula—is it not?

POLITICIAN. —Yes, it is. And this formula, in its coming and not far distant realization, will stand for a much greater achievement in the real progress of culture than it may seem to do at present. Merely reflect on what an amount of evil will die an inevitable death, and what an amount of good will appear and grow, owing to the very nature of things. What great powers will be released for productive work, what progress will be seen in science and art, industry and trade!

MR. Z. —And do you include in the coming achievements of culture a total extinction of diseases and death?

POLITICIAN.—Of course, to some extent. Quite a good deal has already been done in the way of sanitation, hygienics, antiseptics . . . organo–therapeutics . . .

MR. Z.—But do these undoubted triumphs on the positive side really balance the undoubted increase of the symptoms of degeneracy in the spheres of neuropathology and psychopathology, symptoms which accompany the advance of civilization?

POLITICIAN.—Well, in what sort of scales is that to be weighed?

MR. Z.—At any rate, it is absolutely certain that though the *plus* may grow, the *minus* grows as well, and the result obtained is something very near to *nil.* That is the balance-sheet as regards diseases. And as to death, it seems nothing but *nil* has ever been obtained in the progress of culture.

POLITICIAN.—But the progress of culture never sets before itself such an objective as the extinction of death.

MR. Z.—I know it does not. And for this reason it cannot itself be rated very high. Just suppose I know for certain that I myself and all that is dear to me are to disappear for ever. Would it not in such a case be quite immaterial to me whether somewhere in the world certain races are fighting with each other, or whether they live in peace; whether they are civilized or savage, polite or impolite?

POLITICIAN.—Yes, from a personal, egoistical point of view, certainly it would be all the same.

MR. Z.—Why only of egotism? Pardon me, it would be immaterial from any point of view. Death equalizes everything, and in face of it egotism and altruism are equally senseless.

POLITICIAN.—Let it be so. But the senselessness of egotism does not prevent us from being egotists. Similarly, altruism, so far as it is possible at all, can do quite well without any good reasons, and all your argument about death does not touch it in any way.

I am aware that my children and grandchildren are destined to die, but this does not interfere with my efforts to ensure their well-being just as much as if it were to be permanent. I exert myself for their benefit because, in the first place, I love them, and it gives me a moral satisfaction to devote my life to them. "I find a certain gusto in it." It is as clear as daylight.

LADY.—Yes, so long as all goes well—though even then the thought of death comes in all the same. Now, how about the time when various misfortunes begin with the children and grandchildren? What satisfaction and what gusto then? It is just like the water lily in the swamp—you get hold of one and go to the bottom yourself.

MR. Z.—Yes, and besides this, in the case of children and grandchildren, it is of the very nature of things that you take care of them *quand meme,* not waiting to solve or even consider the question as to whether your care can afford them real and final good. You take trouble about them not for some end, but *because* you love them so dearly.

A mankind which is not yet in existence cannot excite such love, and here the question put by our intellect as to the *final* meaning or the object of our cares acquires its full importance. If the answer to this question is death, if the final result of your progress and your culture is but the death of one and all, it is then clear that every kind of activity for the cause of progress and civilization is for no purpose and has no sense.

(Here Mr. Z. interrupted his speech, and all those present turned their heads to the gate which clicked, and for a few seconds they remained in attitudes of inquiry. There they saw the Prince, who had entered the garden and was walking with an unsteady gait towards them.)

LADY. —Oh! And we have not even started the discussion about the Anti–Christ.

PRINCE. —It makes no difference. I have changed my mind, as I think I should not have shown an ill–feeling to the errors of my neighbors before I had heard their plea.

LADY.— *(in a triumphant voice to the General)*. You see! What will you say now?

GENERAL.— *(sharply)*. Nothing!

MR. Z. You have arrived just in time. We are discussing the question whether it is worth while to trouble about progress if we know that the end of it is always death for every man, be he a savage or the highly educated European of the future. What have your theories to say to this?

PRINCE. The true Christian doctrine does not even admit of stating the question in this fashion. The solution of this problem as given in the Gospels "found its most striking and forceful expression in the parable of the Husbandmen.

The husbandmen came to imagine that the garden, to which they had been sent to work for their lord, was their own property; that everything that was in the garden was made for them; and that the only thing they had to do was to enjoy their life in that garden, while giving no thought to its lord, and killing everybody who dared to remind them of his existence and of their duties towards him. Like those husbandmen, so nearly all people in our time live in the absurd belief that they themselves are the lords of their life and that it has been given them for their enjoyment.

The absurdity of this is obvious. For if we have been sent here, this was done at someone's behest and for some purpose. We have, however, decided that we are like mushrooms: that we were born and now live only for our own pleasure; and it is clear that it is as bad for us as it would be bad for the workman who does not carry out his master's will.

But the master's will found its expression in the teaching of Christ. Let people only carry out this teaching, and the Kingdom of God will be established on earth and men will obtain the greatest good that they are capable of securing. All is in that. Seek for the Kingdom of God, and His truth and the rest will come to you of itself. We seek for *the rest* and do not find it; and not only do we not establish the Kingdom of God, but we actually destroy it"[25] by our various States, armies, courts, universities, and factories.

GENERAL *(aside)*. Now the machine has been wound up.

POLITICIAN *(to the Prince)*. Have you finished?

PRINCE. Yes, I have.

POLITICIAN. I must tell you that your solution of the question seems to me absolutely incomprehensible. You seemingly argue about something, try to prove and to explain something, desire to convince us of something, and yet what you say is all a series of arbitrary and mutually disconnected statements.

You say, for instance: "If we have been sent here, this was done at someone's behest and for some purpose." This seems to be your main idea. But what is it? Where did you learn that we have been sent here for a definite purpose? Who told you this? That we exist here on the earth—this is an indisputable fact; but that our existence is some sort of ambassadorship—this you have no ground whatever for asserting.

When, for example, I was in my younger days an ambassador, I knew this for certain, as I also knew by whom and for what I was sent—firstly, because I had incontestable documents stating it; secondly, because I had a personal audience of the late Emperor, Alexander II, and received in person instructions from his Imperial Majesty; and, thirdly, because every quarter I was paid ten thousand rubles in gold.

Now, if instead of all that some stranger had come up to me in the street and said that I was made an ambassador to be sent to some place, for some purpose or other—well, I should at once have looked round to see if I could find a policeman who would protect me from a maniac, capable, perhaps, even of committing an assault on my person.

As regards the present case, you will admit that you have no incontestable documents from your supposed Lord, that you have had no personal audience with Him and that no salary is being paid to you. And you call yourself an ambassador! Why, not only yourself, but even

---

[25] Quotation from Tolstoy. (Translator.)

everybody in existence you have declared to be either an ambassador or a husbandman. Have you any right to make such statements? Or any ground? No, I refuse to understand it. It seems to me a kind of rhetorical improvisation *très mal inspirée d'ailleurs.*

LADY.—Again pretending ignorance! How bad of you! You understand quite well that the Prince was not trying at all to refute your unbelief, but was stating the commonly accepted Christian opinion that we all depend on God and are obliged to serve Him.

POLITICIAN.—No, I cannot understand a service without a salary. And if it proves that the salary here is one and the same for everybody— death, well then, I present my compliments. . . .

LADY.— But you will die in any case, and nobody will ask for your consent.

POLITICIAN. Anyhow! Yes, and that proves that life is not service, and if my assent is not required for my death, any more than for my birth, then I prefer to look upon death, as also life, as being merely a necessity of Nature and not to bring in the idea of some sort of service to some unknown master. So my conclusion is this: Live while you can, and strive to live as wisely and well as possible; and the condition of a wise and good life is peaceful culture. However, I am of the opinion that even on the basis of the Christian doctrine the sham solution of the problem, suggested by the Prince, will not stand the slightest criticism. But let the others, more competent than myself, speak of this.

GENERAL.— Of course, it is not a solution at all. It is merely a verbal way of getting round the question. Just as if I took a map and, having surrounded with my penciled battalions an enemy's penciled fortress, imagined then that I actually took the actual fortress. Things of this kind did really happen, you know, as the popular soldiers' song tells :

> "The Devil carried off a quarter of us
> As we were taking the heights.
>
> The princes and the counts came,
> The surveyors made their maps
> On great sheets of foolscap.
> It all looked smooth on paper,
>
> But they forgot the precipices,
> And how to get across them."

The result of which is well known.

> " At the heights of Thediuchin
> But two companies of us arrived,
> The regiments disappeared."

PRINCE.—This is all beyond me! Is this all that you can reply to what I said?

GENERAL.—But the point which seemed to me particularly unintelligible in what you said, was the matter of the mushrooms, as though they live for their own pleasure. I have always supposed that they live for the pleasure of those who like mushrooms in sour cream, or a mushroom pie. Now, if your Kingdom of God on earth leaves death untouched, then it follows that people will have no choice about living, and in your Kingdom of God they will live precisely as mushrooms—not the joyful imaginary mushrooms that you suppose, but real mushrooms which are cooked in a pan. Similarly for people in your earthly Kingdom of God, everything will end one way, namely, death will devour them.

LADY.—The Prince did not say that.

GENERAL.—Neither so, nor otherwise. But what is the reason of such a reticence concerning the most important point?

MR. Z.—Before taking up this question, I should like to know what was the source of the parable in which you, Prince, expressed your view? Or is it your own composition?

PRINCE.—Composition, indeed! You know it comes from the Gospel.

MR. Z.—No, not so! There is no such parable found in any of the Gospels.

LADY.—Heaven help you! Why do you distort the Prince's meaning? You know there is the parable of the husbandmen in the Gospel.

MR. Z.—Superficially it is somewhat like it, but altogether different both in tenor and meaning, which is immediately thereafter pointed out.

LADY. Oh, no, surely not! I think it is exactly the same parable. Oh, you are trying to be too clever, I notice—I don't trust a single word of yours.

MR. Z.—You needn't; I have the book in my pocket. *(Here he took out a small pocket copy of the New Testament and began to turn over the pages.)* The parable of the husbandman can be found given by three evangelists: Saints Matthew, Mark, and Luke, but all of them state it in very much the same form. It will, therefore, be sufficient to quote it from the more elaborate Gospel of St. Luke.

It is in Chapter 20 in which the last sermon of Christ to the people is given. The drama was nearing its end, and it is now narrated (end of Chapter 19 and beginning of Chapter 20.) how the enemies of Christ—the party of chief priests and scribes made an open and decisive attack on Him, demanding publicly that He should state His authority and explain by what right and in virtue of what power He was acting. But I think I had better read it to you. *(Reads.)*

"And He taught daily in the Temple. But the chief priests and the scribes and the chief of the people sought to destroy Him. And could not find what they might do; for all the people were very attentive to hear Him. And it came to pass, that on one of those days, as He taught the people in the Temple, and preached the Gospel, the chief priests and the scribes came upon Him with the elders. And spake unto Him, saying: Tell us, by what authority doest Thou these things? or who is He that gave Thee this authority?

And He answered and said unto them, I will also ask you one thing, and answer Me: The baptism of John, was it from Heaven or of men? And they reasoned with themselves, saying, If we shall say, From Heaven, He will say, Why then believed ye Him not? But and if we say, Of men, all the people will stone us; for they be persuaded that John was a prophet. And they answered, that they could not tell whence it was: And Jesus said unto them, Neither tell I you by what authority I do these things. . . ."

LADY.—And why do you read all this? It was quite right of Christ not to answer when he was worried by these men. But what has it to do with the husbandmen?

MR. Z.— A little patience: it all leads to the same thing. Besides, you are mistaken when you say that Christ did not answer. He answered most definitely —and twice over: quoted such a witness of His authority as the questioners dared not reject, and next proved that they themselves had no proper authority or right over Him, as they acted only out of fear of the people, afraid for their lives, adapting themselves to the opinions of the mob. But real authority is that which does not follow others, but itself leads them forward.

Fearing and obeying the people, these men revealed that the real authority had deserted them and belonged to the people. It is to these latter that Christ now addresses Himself in order to accuse them of resisting Him. In this accusation of the unworthy leaders of the Jewish nation for their resistance to the Messiah—there lies all the story of the gospel parable of the husbandmen, as you will presently see for yourself. *(Reads):*

"Then began He to speak to the people this parable: A certain man planted a vineyard, and let it forth to husbandmen, and went into a far country for a long time. And at the season he sent a servant to the husbandmen, that they should give him of the fruit of the vineyard: but the husbandmen beat him, and sent him away empty. And again he sent another servant, and they beat him also, and entreated him shamefully, and sent him away empty. And again he sent a third: and they wounded him also, and cast him out.

Then said the lord of the vineyard, What shall I do? I will send my beloved son: it may be they will reverence him when they see him. But when the husbandmen saw him, they reasoned among themselves, saying, This is the heir: come, let us kill him, that the inheritance may be ours. So they cast him out of the vineyard, and killed him. What, therefore, shall the lord of the vineyard do unto them? He shall come and destroy these husbandmen and shall give the vineyard to others. And when they heard it, they said, God forbid.

And He beheld them and said, What is this then that is written, The stone which the builders rejected, the same is become the head of the corner? Whosoever shall fall upon that stone shall be broken; but on whomsoever it shall fall, it will grind him to powder. And the chief priests and the scribes that same hour sought to lay hands on Him; for they feared the people: for they perceived that He had spoken this parable against them." About whom, then, and about what, I ask you, was the parable of the vineyard told?

PRINCE.— I can't understand what it is you are driving at. The Judean chief priests and scribes felt offended because they were, and knew themselves to be, the representatives of those wicked lay people of which the parable spoke.

MR. Z.—But of what was it they were accused in the parable?

PRINCE.—Of not carrying out the true teaching.

POLITICIAN.—I think the whole thing is clear enough. The scoundrels lived like mushrooms for their own enjoyment, smoked tobacco, drank spirits, ate slaughtered meat, and also offered of it to their god: besides which, they got married, presided in law courts, and engaged in warfare.

LADY.—Do you think that it is worthy of your age and position to indulge in such sneering outbursts? Do not listen to him, Prince. We want to speak seriously with you.

Tell me this. in the Gospel parable, you know, the husbandmen were destroyed because they murdered the owner's son and heir — and this is the main point in the Gospel—why do you omit it?

PRINCE.—I leave it out for the simple reason that it refers to the personal fate of Christ, which, naturally, has its own importance and interest, but is, after all, inessential to that which is one and the same for everybody.

LADY.—That is?

PRINCE.— The carrying out of the Gospel teaching, by means of which the Kingdom of God and His justice are attained.

LADY.—Wait a moment; I have everything all confused in my head— what exactly is it?—Yes *(to Mr. Z.)*, you have the Gospel in your hands, so tell us, please, what comes in this chapter after the parable?

MR. Z.—*(turning over the pages of the little book)*. It is also stated there that it is necessary that those things which be Caesar's should be rendered to Caesar; that the dead will be raised, because God is not a God of the dead, but of the living, and there is further given a proof that Christ is not David's son, but the Son of God. Then the last two verses are against the hypocrisy and vanity of the Scribes.

LADY.—There, you see, Prince! And this also is Gospel teaching; that we must acknowledge the state in worldly matters, we must believe in the resurrection of the dead, and also that Christ is not a mere man but the Son of God.

PRINCE.—But how can it be possible to conclude this from one chapter of uncertain authorship and date?

LADY.— Oh, no! This I know even without looking up the matter in books, that not only in a single chapter, but in all the four Gospels, a great deal is said both about resurrection and about Christ's divinity— particularly in St. John's Gospel, which is even read at funeral services.

MR. Z.—As to the uncertainty of the origin of the Gospels, it is now recognized, even by the liberal German critics, that all the four Gospels were composed in the time of the Apostles, that is, in the first century.

POLITICIAN.—Why, even the thirteenth edition of *"La Vie de Jesus"* I have noticed contains a retraction of what had originally been said about the fourth gospel.

MR. Z.—One must not lag behind one's teachers. But the principal difficulty, Prince, is that whatever our four Gospels may be, whenever and by whomsoever they were composed, there is no other gospel extant more trustworthy and more in agreement with your teaching than this.

GENERAL.—Who told you it does not exist? Why, there is the fifth one, which contains nothing of Christ but the *teaching*—about slaughtered meat and military service.

LADY.—And you also? You should be ashamed of yourself. Remember that the more you and your civil ally tease the Prince, the more support I shall give him myself. I am sure, Prince, that you want to look upon Christianity from its best side, and that your gospel, though not the same as ours, is similar to the books composed in times gone by: something like "L'Esprit de M. de Montesquieu," "L'Esprit de Fénélon," etc. In the same way, you or your teachers wanted to compose "L'Esprit de l'Evangile."

It is only a great pity that nobody of your persuasion has done it in a small book, which could be called *"The Spirit of Christianity* according to the teaching of so–and–so." You should have some sort of a catechism, so that we simple folk should not lose the thread in all your variations. One moment we are told that the whole thing is in the Sermon on the Mount; another moment that we must first of all labor in the sweat of our brow in agricultural work—though the Gospel does not say this anywhere.

Genesis does, however, in the part where it also speaks of giving birth in pains—this, however, not being a commandment, but only a grievous necessity. Then we are told that we must give everything we have to the poor, and the next moment that we must not give anything to anybody, since money is evil, and it is bad to do evil to others, save to ourselves and our family; whilst for the rest we must work.

Then again we are told to do nothing but contemplate. Yet again, that the mission of women is to give birth to as many healthy children as possible, and then suddenly that nothing of the kind is necessary. Then that we must not eat meat—this is the first stage, and why the first nobody can tell. We must give up now spirits and smoking, now pancakes. Last comes the objection to military service—that all evil is due to it, and that the first duty of a Christian is to refuse doing it; and whoever has not been officially recruited is, of course, holy as he is. Perhaps I am talking nonsense, but this is not my fault—it is absolutely impossible for me to make head or tail of all this.

PRINCE.—I also think that we require a sensible summary of the true teaching—I believe it is being prepared now.

LADY.—Well, and while it is being prepared, tell us now briefly what is the essence of the Gospel in your opinion.

PRINCE.— Surely it is clear enough: it is the great principle of the non–resistance of evil by force.

POLITICIAN.— And how do you deduce from this the smoking?

PRINCE.— What smoking?

POLITICIAN.— Oh, dear me! I ask what connection is there between the principle of the non–resistance of evil and the rules of abstinence from tobacco, wine, meat, and sexual intercourse?

PRINCE. —The connection, I think, is clear: all these vicious habits stupefy a man—they overpower in him the demands of his reason or conscience. This is why soldiers generally go off drunk to war.

MR. Z.— Particularly to an unsuccessful war. But we may leave this alone. The rule of not resisting evil has its own importance apart from the question whether it justifies ascetic life or does not. According to you, if we do not resist evil by force, evil will immediately disappear. It follows that evil exists only by our resistance or by those measures which we take against it, but has no real power of its own. Properly speaking, there is no evil existing at all, and it appears only owing to our erroneous belief that it does exist and that we begin to act in accordance with the presumption. Isn't it so?

PRINCE.— No doubt it is.

MR. Z.— But if there is no evil existing in reality how will you explain the startling failure of Christ's cause in history? From your point of view, it has, of course, proved an utter failure, so that no good results can be credited to it, whilst the harm done has undoubtedly far exceeded its good effects.

PRINCE. —How so?

MR. Z.— A strange question to ask, to be sure! Well, if you do not understand it we will examine it in a methodical manner. You agree that Christ preached true good in a more clear, powerful, and consistent way than anybody else, didn't He?

PRINCE.—Yes, He did.

MR. Z.—And true good consists in not opposing evil with force, that is, so–called evil, since there is no actual evil.

PRINCE.—Yes.

MR. Z.— Christ not only preached, but carried out to the last end the demands of this good by suffering without any resistance the torments of crucifixion. Christ, according to you, died and did not rise. Very well. Thousands of His followers suffered the same. Very well again. But now, what has been the result of it all?

PRINCE.— Would you like to see all these martyrs, as a reward of their deeds, crowned by angels with brilliant wreaths and reclining somewhere under the trees in Elysian gardens?

MR. Z.— Oh no, there is no need to take it that way. Of course we all, including yourself, I hope, wish all that is best and most pleasant to our neighbors, both living and dead. But the question is not of our wishes, but of what has actually resulted from the preaching and sacrifice of Christ and His followers.

PRINCE.— Resulted for whom? For themselves?

MR. Z.— What resulted for themselves everybody knows: a painful death. But moral heroes as they were, they willingly accepted it, not in order to get brilliant wreaths for themselves, but to secure true benefit for others, the whole of mankind. Now I ask you, what are the benefits earned by mankind through their martyrdom? In the words of an old saying, "The blood of martyrs is the seed of the Church!' In point of fact, it is quite true. But your contention is that the Church has been nothing but the distortion and ruin of true Christianity, which was, as a result, entirely forgotten by mankind, so that it became necessary to restore everything from the very beginning without any guarantee for any greater success; in other words, quite hopelessly.

PRINCE.—Why hopelessly?

MR. Z.— Because you have admitted yourself that Christ and the first generations of Christians gave all their thoughts and sacrificed their lives for their cause, and if, this notwithstanding, nothing resulted from their efforts, what grounds have you then for hoping for any other result?

There is only one indubitable and permanent end to all such practice of good, the same for those who initiated it, and for those who distorted and ruined it, and for those who have been restoring it. They all, according to you, died in the past, die in the present, will die in the future. And from the practice of good, the preaching of truth, nothing but death ever came, comes, or promises to come. Well, what is the meaning of it all? Isn't it strange: the non–existent evil always triumphs and the good always falls through to nothingness?

LADY.—Do not evil people die as well?

MR. Z.— Very much so. But the point is that the power of evil is only *confirmed* by the reign of death, whereas the power of good would, on the contrary, be disproved. Indeed, evil is *obviously* more powerful than good, and if the *obvious* is the only thing real, then you cannot but admit that the world is the work of the evil power.

How some people, whilst recognizing only the obvious reality, and therefore admitting the predominance of evil over good, maintain at the same time that evil does not exist, and that consequently there is no need for fighting it—this passes my understanding, and I expect the Prince to help me in this difficulty.

POLITICIAN.—Well, to begin with, tell us your way out of the difficulty.

MR. Z.— It is quite simple. Evil really exists, and it finds its expression not only in the deficiency of good, but in the positive resistance and predominance of the lower qualities over the higher ones in all the spheres of Being. There is an individual evil—when the lower side of men, the animal and bestial passions, resist the better impulses of the soul, *overpowering* them, in the great majority of people.

There is a social evil, when the human crowd, individually enslaved by evil, resists the salutary efforts of the few better men and eventually overpowers them. There is, lastly, a physical evil in man, when the baser material constituents of his body resist the living and enlightening power which binds them up together in a beautiful form of organism—resist and break the form, destroying the real basis of the higher life. This is the *extreme* evil, called death. And had we been compelled to recognize the victory of this extreme physical evil as final and absolute, then no imaginary victories of good in the individual and social spheres could be considered real successes.

Let us, indeed, imagine that a good man, say Socrates, not only triumphed over his inner forces—the bad passions—but also succeeded in convincing and reforming his social foes, in reconstructing the Hellenic "politeia." Now what would be the use of this ephemeral and superficial victory over evil if it is allowed finally to triumph in the deepest strata of Being over the very foundations of life? Because, both for the reformer and for the reformed there is but one end: death.

By what logic would it be possible to appraise highly the moral victories of Socrates' good over the moral microbes of bad passions within him and over the social microbes of the Athenian *agora,* if the real victors would after all be the much worse, baser, and coarser microbes of physical decomposition? Here no moral verbiage will protect you against utter pessimism and despair.

POLITICIAN.— We have heard this before. What is your remedy against despair?

MR. Z.— Our remedy is one: actual resurrection. We know that the struggle between good and evil is not confined only to soul or society, but is carried on in the deeper spheres of the physical world. We already have recorded in the past one victory of the good power of life—the personal resurrection of One, and we are looking forward to future victories of the congregate resurrection of all.

Here even evil is given its reason or the final explanation of its existence in that it serves to enhance the triumph, realization, and power of good: if death is more powerful than mortal life, resurrection to external life is even more powerful than both of them. The Kingdom of God is the kingdom of life triumphing through resurrection—in which life there lies the real, actual, and final good. In this rests all the power and work of Christ, in this His real love to us and ours to Him; whereas all the other things are only the condition, the path, the preliminary steps.

Without the faith in the accomplished resurrection of One, and without cherishing the future resurrection of all men, all talk of some Kingdom of God remains nothing but words, whilst in reality one finds only the Kingdom of Death.

PRINCE.—How is that?

MR. Z.— Why, because you not only admit with everybody else the *fact* of death as such, that is that men generally died, die, and will die, but you raise this fact to the position of an absolute law, which does not in your opinion permit of a single exception. But what should we call the world in which death for ever has the force of an absolute law but the Kingdom of Death? And what is your Kingdom of God on Earth but an arbitrary and purposeless euphemism for the Kingdom of Death?

POLITICIAN.—I also think it is purposeless, because it is wrong to replace a known quantity by an unknown one. Nobody has seen God and nobody knows what His Kingdom may be. But we have all seen the death of men and animals, and we also know that nobody in the world can escape this supreme power of death. What is the good then of replacing this certain "a" by some unknown "x"? Nothing but confusion and temptation for the "little ones" will ever result from such a substitution.

PRINCE.—I do not quite understand what we are now discussing. Death is a phenomenon, certainly very interesting, you can if you like call it a law, as being a phenomenon constant amongst earthly creatures and unavoidable by any of them; you can also speak of the absoluteness of that law, since, hitherto, there has been no clearly established exception; but what real or vital importance can all that have for the true Christian teaching, which speaks to us through our conscience only about one thing: namely, what we ought and what we ought not to do *here* and *now?*

It is clear that the voice of conscience can refer only to that which it is in our power to do or not to do. Therefore, conscience not only says nothing to us about death, but cannot say anything. With all its immense importance for our human earthly feelings and desires, death is not subject to our will and therefore it cannot have any moral importance for us. In that respect—and that is the only thing of importance at the moment—death is a purely indifferent fact, just as much as bad weather, for example. Because I acknowledge the inevitable periodical occurrence of bad weather and more or less suffer from it, am I therefore bound to say, instead of the Kingdom of God, the kingdom of bad weather?

MR. Z.—No, you are not; in the first place, because bad weather has its kingdom only in St. Petersburg and we have come here with you to the Mediterranean and laugh at its kingdom; and secondly, your simile does not fit because one can praise God even in bad weather and feel one's self in His Kingdom, while the dead, as is said in the Scriptures, praise not God; also because, as his Excellency remarked, it is more suitable to call this sorrowful world the kingdom of death than the Kingdom of God.

LADY.—Why are you arguing all the time about titles? It is so uninteresting. Titles, surely, matter very little. You had better tell me, Prince, what you actually understand by the Kingdom of God and His Righteousness.

PRINCE.— By this I understand the state of men when they act only in accordance with their inner conscience and thus carry out the will of God, which prescribes them nothing but pure good.

MR. Z.— The voice of conscience, however, speaks of performing what is due only *now* and *here.* Isn't this the view you hold?

PRINCE.— You are quite correct.

MR. Z.— But does your conscience remain silent about those wicked deeds which you may have committed in your youth in relation to people long since dead?

PRINCE.—In such cases, the point of these reminders is that I should not do anything of that sort *now.*

MR. Z.—Well, that's not quite so, but it's not worth while quarrelling about. I only want to remind you of another and more incontestable sphere of conscience. Long ago the moralists compared the voice of conscience to that genius or demon which accompanied Socrates warning him against undutiful conduct, but never pointing out positively what he ought to do. Exactly the same thing may be said of conscience.

PRINCE.— How is that? Does not conscience suggest to me, say, that I should help my neighbor in case of need or danger?

MR. Z.— I am very glad to hear this from you. But, if you analyze carefully such a position you will see that the *role* of conscience, even here, proves to be entirely negative; it demands of you merely that you should not remain inactive or indifferent in face of someone else's need, but how precisely you ought to act on his behalf, conscience itself does not tell you.

PRINCE.—Just so, because this depends on the circumstances of the case, on my position and on that of the man ought to help.

MR. Z.—Of course, but the weighing and appraising of these circumstances and conditions is not the business of the conscience but of the mind.

PRINCE.— How can you separate reason from conscience?

MR. Z.— You need not separate them, but you must distinguish them. Because just in reality it sometimes happens that reason and conscience become not only separated but even opposed to each other. Should they be one and the same thing, how would it then be possible for reason to be used for acts not only foreign to morality, but positively immoral?

And, you know, this does happen. Why, even help can be offered in a way that is approved by reason but is inimical to moral consciousness. For instance, I may give food and drink and show other consideration to a needy man in order only to make him an accomplice in a fraud I am preparing, or any other wicked act.

PRINCE.— Well, it is, of course, so elementary. But what conclusion do you deduce from it?

MR. Z.—Why this. If the voice of conscience, with all its proper significance as a warner and reproacher, does not give positive practical and definite directions for our action, and our free will stands in need of the mind as an assisting instrument, and if meanwhile the mind shows: itself to be a doubtful servant for it, since it is capable and ready to serve two masters—good and evil—then for the fulfillment of the will of God and the attaining of the Kingdom of God, besides the conscience and reason, yet a certain third thing is necessary.

PRINCE.—What is that in your opinion?

MR. Z.—To put it shortly, it is the *inspiration of good,* or a direct and positive action of the best principle upon us and in us. In such a joint action, both reason and conscience become trusty helpers of the good itself, and morality, instead of being a good behavior, which is always questionable, becomes an unquestionable life lived in the good itself—becomes the organic development and completion of the whole of man—within and without, individual and society, people and mankind, so as to come to its climax in a living unity formed of the revived past together with the evolving future in the eternal present of the Kingdom of God, which will indeed be on earth, but only on a new earth which is lovingly united to a new heaven.

PRINCE.—I have nothing against such poetical metaphors, but why do you suppose that people who are fulfilling the will of God according to the Gospel commandments lack what you call the inspiration of good?

MR. Z.— They are not; not only because I do not see in their actions any signs of such an inspiration, of those free and sweeping impulses of love (God does not measure out the spirit He gives to man); nor only because I do not see that joyous and compliant peace arising from possessing those gifts, if even only primary ones, do I fail to see in you the religious inspiration, but because, properly speaking, you yourself recognize its uselessness for you. If good is confined only to carrying out the "rule," there is no room left here for inspiration.

Is there? A "rule" is given once and for all, is definite and the same for everybody. He who gave that rule has been dead long since, and, according to you, has never risen to life, so that He has not for us any personal vital existence. Whilst at the same time you see the absolute, primary good, not as a father of light and life, who could breathe light and life straight into you, but as a prudent lord, who sent you, his hirelings, to do the work in his vineyard, while he himself lives somewhere abroad and sends his men to you to bring him his rent.

PRINCE.— We did not invent that image arbitrarily.

MR. Z.—No, but you arbitrarily see in it the highest force of the relation between man and God in arbitrarily excluding from the Gospel text the very substance of it. Which is to point to the son and heir in whom is found the true living type of the relation between God and man. It is a case of a master, obligations to a master, and the will of a master. But this is what I have to say to you in reply: As long as your lord only imposes duties on you and demands from you compliance with his will, I do not see how you can prove to me that he is a true lord and not an impostor.

PRINCE.—That's very nice, and supposing I know, both in conscience and reason, that the demands of the lord are simply expressive of the purest form of good.

MR. Z.—I am sorry; I am not speaking of that. I do not dispute that the lord demands good of you; but does it follow that he is himself good?

PRINCE.— What else could he be?

MR. Z.—How strange. I always thought that the quality of goodness in anybody is not shown by what he demands of others but by what he does himself. If this is not clear to you logically, then here's an actual historical example for you. The Moscow Tsar, Ivan the Terrible, in his well-known letter, demanded of Prince Andrew Kurbsky that he should display the greatest good and highest moral heroism by refusing resistance to evil and simply submitting himself to a martyr's death for the truth. This will of the lord was good in what it demanded of another, only it did not in any way prove that the lord who demanded such good was himself good. It is clear that, although martyrdom for the truth is the highest moral good, yet this does not imply anything in defense of Ivan the Terrible, seeing that he was in this instance not the martyr but the cause of martyrdom.

PRINCE.— Perhaps. But what do you want to prove by this?

MR. Z.—I mean, that so long as you do not show me the good quality of your lord in his own deeds, but only in his verbal instructions to his workmen, I remain of my opinion that this far-away master of yours, demanding good of others, but doing nothing good himself, imposing obligation, but showing no love, never appearing for you to see, but living somewhere away *incognito*—that he is none other than the *God of this world* . . .

GENERAL. Here it is, this damned *incognito!*

LADY.—Ah, do not say so! How terrible! The Power of the Cross defend us. (She crosses herself.)

PRINCE.—It was possible earlier on to foresee something of this kind.

MR. Z.—I have no doubt, Prince, that you, are genuinely erring, when you accept a clever impostor for the true God. The *cleverness* of the impostor is, for you, a great extenuating circumstance; I myself have not analyzed how the matter stands; but at present I have no doubt whatever, and you will understand with what feelings I must regard what I consider to be a deceitful and seductive *mask* of good.

LADY.—Oh, how can you say this. It hurts one's feelings.

PRINCE.—I assure you I am not in the least offended. A general and very interesting question was put, and it is strange to me that my opponent apparently imagines that this question has to do with me only, and not with himself as well. You demand of me that I should show you the really good deeds of my master, which are witnesses of the fact that he is the origin of good and not evil. Well, will you yourselves show me any good deed of your master which I would not be able to ascribe to mine?

GENERAL. You have already heard of one such deed, by which all the rest stand.

PRINCE.—What exactly?

MR. Z.—The real victory over evil in the real resurrection. Only by this, I repeat, is revealed the true Kingdom of God. For without that there is only the kingdom of death and sin, and of their creator, the Devil. The resurrection—only not in a figurative sense, but in a real one—that is the proof of the true God.

PRINCE.—Yes, if it pleases you to believe in such mythology. I, you know, ask you for facts which are capable of proof and not for your beliefs.

MR. Z.—Not so fast, Prince. We both start from the same belief, or, if you like, mythology, with this difference—that I consistently carry it through to its logical end; whilst you, violating logic, arbitrarily stop at the first stage. After all, you do recognize the power of good and its coming triumph over evil, don't you?

PRINCE.— Most emphatically!

MR. Z.— But what is it: a fact or a belief?

PRINCE.— A *reasonable* belief.

MR. Z.—Let us see. Reason, as we were taught in the Seminary, demands, among other things, that nothing is to be accepted without sufficient grounds. Now tell me what sufficient grounds have you, whilst admitting the power that good has in the moral development and perfection of man and mankind, not to admit that power against death?

PRINCE.— In my opinion it is for you to answer why you attribute to good some power beyond the limits of the moral sphere.

MR. Z.— Oh, I can answer that. If I believe in good and its own power, whilst assuming in the very notion of good its essential and *absolute* superiority, then I am bound by logic to recognize that power as unlimited, and nothing can prevent me from believing in the truth of resurrection, which is *historically* testified.

However, if you had said frankly from the very beginning that the Christian *faith* was nothing to you, that its matter was mythological to you, then I, of course, should have restrained myself from expressing that animosity to your manner of thought, which I was not able to hide from you.

For bearing animosity towards people for their theoretical fallacies and errors means acknowledging oneself to be small in mind, weak in faith and wretched at heart. But everybody really religious, and thereby freed from these extremes of stupidity, cowardice, and heartlessness, must look with real good will at a straightforward, frank, in a word, *honest* opponent and denier of religious truths.

It is so rare to meet such a one in our time, and it is even difficult for me to describe to you how greatly I am pleased when I see an open enemy of Christianity. In nearly everyone of them I am inclined to see a future St. Paul, whilst in some of the zealots of Christianity there seem to be looming Judas, the traitor himself. But you, Prince, have now stated your opinion so frankly that I positively refuse to include you amongst the innumerable Judases and little Judases of our time. I can even foresee the moment when I shall feel towards you the same kind disposition of humor which I experience when meeting out–and–out atheists and infidels.

POLITICIAN.—Well, since now it is so happily explained that neither these atheists and infidels nor such "true Christians" as the Prince here represent Antichrist, the time has come at last for you to show us his real portrait.

MR. Z.— You want rather too much, your Excellency. Are you satisfied, for instance, with a single one of all the innumerable portraits of Christ which, you will admit, have sometimes been made even by artists of genius? Personally, I don't know of a single satisfactory portrait. I believe such is even impossible, for Christ is an individual, unique in His own kind and in the personification of His essence—good. To paint it, a genius will not suffice.

The same, moreover, has to be said about Anti–Christ: he is also an individual, singular in completeness and finish, a personification of evil. It is impossible to show his portrait. In Church literature we find only his passport with a description of his general and some special marks . . .

LADY.— No; we do not want his portrait, God save us! You had better explain why he himself is necessary in your opinion, what his work really is, and if he will come soon.

MR. Z.—Well, I am able to satisfy you better than you think. Some years ago one of my fellow-students in the Church Academy, who afterwards became a monk, on his deathbed, bequeathed to me a manuscript of his which he valued highly, but was unwilling and unable to print. He calls it, "A Short Story about Antichrist." Though dressed in the form of fiction, as an imaginary forecast of the historical future, this paper, in my opinion, gives all that could be said on this subject in accordance with the Bible, with Church tradition, and the dictates of sound sense.

POLITICIAN.—Is it the work of our old friend Monk Varsanophius?

MR. Z.—No, his name was one of far more refinement, Pansophius.

POLITICIAN.—Pan Sophius. Was he a Pole?

MR. Z.—Not at all; a son of one of the Russian priests. If you will permit me to go up to my room for a moment I will fetch the manuscript and read it to you. It isn't long.

LADY.—Make haste, make haste! See that you don't get lost! (While Mr. Z. goes to his room for the manuscript all get up and walk about the garden.)

POLITICIAN.—I do not know what it is; either my eyesight is dimmed by old age, or something has happened in nature. Only, I notice that there are now no longer in any season, or in any place, any more of those bright and quite clear days, which formerly there were in all climates. Take today; not a cloud; we are far enough from the sea, and yet everything as it were, is covered with something—something fine and intangible, and there is no absolute clearness. Have you noticed it, General?

GENERAL.—I have noticed it for many years.

LADY.—And I, for this past year, have begun to notice it also. Not only in the air but in the soul: for here there is no "absolute clearness," as you say. Everywhere there is some sort of alarm, as if it were a foreboding of some evil. I am sure that you, Prince, feel the same thing.

PRINCE.—No, I have noticed nothing special. The air seems as usual.

GENERAL.—But you are too young to notice any difference. You have no means of comparison. How can you remember? But when you look back over fifty years you feel something.

PRINCE.—I think the first supposition is correct. It is a phenomenon of weak eyesight.

POLITICIAN.—We are growing old undoubtedly; but neither is the earth growing younger; a double weariness is felt.

GENERAL. I think it is even more likely that the Devil, with his tail, is spreading fog over the world. Another sign of the Anti–Christ!

LADY (pointing out Mr. Z., who was descending the terrace).—We shall soon know all about it.

(They all sit down in their former places and Mr. Z. begins to read the manuscript he has brought with him.)

A BRIEF NOVELLA ABOUT ANTICHRIST.

Pan–mongolism! The name is savage,
But it pleases my ear immensely,
A mystical premonition, as it were,
Of the great destiny appointed by God. . . .

LADY.—Where is this motto taken from?

MR. Z.—I think, the author wrote it himself.

LADY.—Well, read on.

MR. Z *(reads)*. The twentieth century A.D. was the epoch of the last great wars and revolutions. The greatest of those wars had its remote cause in the movement of *Pan–Mongolism,* which originated in Japan as far back as the end of the nineteenth century.

The imitative Japanese, who showed such a wonderful cleverness in copying the external forms of European culture, also assimilated certain European ideas of the baser sort. Having learned from the papers and text–books on history that there were in the West such movements as Pan–Hellenism, Pan–Germanism, Pan–Slavism, Pan–Islamism, they proclaimed to the world the great idea of Pan–Mongolism; that is, the unification under their leadership of all the races of Eastern Asia, with the object of conducting a determined warfare against the foreign intruders, that is the Europeans.

Taking advantage of the fact that Europe was engaged in a final and decisive struggle with the Moslem world in the beginning of the twentieth century, they seized the opportunity to attempt the realization of their great plan—first, by occupying Korea, then Peking, where, assisted by the revolutionary party in China, they deposed the old Manchu dynasty and put in its place a Japanese one. In this the Chinese Conservatives soon acquiesced, as they understood that of two evils the less is the better, and that "family ties make all brothers, whether they wish it or not."

The independence of the old Chinese S*tate* proved unable to maintain itself, and subjection to the Europeans or the Japanese became inevitable. It seemed clear, however, that the dominance of the Japanese, though it abolished the external forms of the Chinese state organization (which besides became palpably worthless), did not interfere with the main foundations of the national life, whereas the dominance of the European Powers, which for political reasons supported Christian missionaries, would have threatened the very spiritual basis of China.

The former national hatred of the Chinese for the Japanese had arisen at a time when neither the one nor the other had known Europeans, in the presence of whom this enmity of two related peoples became mere civil dissension, and lost any significance. The Europeans were *unreservedly* alien, *nothing but* enemies, and their predominance promised nothing that could flatter the national ambition, whilst in the hands of Japan the Chinese saw the tempting bait of Pan–Mongolism, which at the same time made more acceptable to their mind the painful necessity of assimilating the external forms of the European culture.

"You see, O obstinate brothers," said the Japanese, "that we take the weapons of the Western dogs, not from any infatuation for them, but simply to beat them with their own devices. If you join us and accept our practical guidance we shall not only quickly drive the white devils our of our Asia, but also to conquer their own lands⁻ and establish the true Middle Empire all the world over.

You are right in your national pride and your contempt for the Europeans, but you should keep these feelings alive not only by dreams, but by sensible actions as well. In this we have surpassed you and we must show you the way of our common welfare. Otherwise, see for yourselves what your policy of self–assurance and distrust of us, your natural friends and defenders, has given you: Russia and England, Germany and France have almost shared you between them, leaving you nothing, and all your tigerish plots show only the weak end of a serpent's tail."

The sensible Chinese found this reasonable, and the Japanese dynasty became firmly established. Its first care was, of course, to create a powerful army and fleet. The greater part of the Japanese troops were brought over to China and served as a nucleus for the new colossal army.

The Japanese officers who could speak Chinese proved much more successful instructors than the dismissed Europeans, whilst the immense population of China, with Manchuria, Mongolia, and Tibet, provided a sufficient supply of good fighting material.

Already the first Chinese Emperor of the Japanese dynasty was able to make a successful trial of the arms of the revived empire, driving out the French from Tonkin and Siam, the English from Burma, and including in the Middle Empire all of Indo–China.

His heir, Chinese on his mother's side, thus uniting in himself both the cunning and elasticity of the Chinese with the energy, mobility and enterprise of the Japanese, mobilized in Chinese Turkestan an army of four millions, and at the time that the Tsun–li–Yamin confidently informed the Russian Ambassador that this force was intended for the conquest of India, the Emperor with his immense forces suddenly invaded Russian Central Asia, and having here raised against us all the population, rapidly crossed the Ural Mountains and overran Eastern and Central Russia with his troops, whilst the Russian armies, mobilized in all haste, were hurrying to meet them from Poland and Lithuania, Kiev and Volhynia, St. Petersburg, and Finland.

Owing to the absence of a prearranged plan of campaign and the enormous numerical superiority of the enemy, the fighting qualities of the Russian forces allow them only to perish with honor. The swiftness of the invasion left no time for the necessary concentration, and army corps after army corps was exterminated in hard and hopeless conflicts. The Mongols did not come off cheaply, but they easily replaced their losses, having control of all the Asiatic railways, while a Russian army of two hundred thousand, for a long time concentrated on the Manchurian frontier, made an unsuccessful attempt to invade a well–defended China.

Having left a part of his forces in Russia to prevent the forming of new armies, and also for the pursuit of guerilla bands which had increased in number, the Emperor with three armies crossed the German frontier. Here the country had had sufficient time to prepare itself, and one of the Mongolian armies met with a crushing defeat. At this time, however, in France the party of belated *revanche* acquired the power, and soon the Germans found in their rear an army of a million bayonets.

Finding itself between the hammer and the anvil, the German Army was compelled to accept the honorable terms of peace offered to it by the Chinese Emperor. The jubilant French fraternizing with the yellow faces were scattered throughout Germany, and soon lost every appearance of military discipline.

The Emperor ordered his army to cut up allies who were no longer useful, and with Chinese punctiliousness the order was exactly carried out. Simultaneously in Paris workmen *sans patrie* organised a rising, and the capital of Western culture joyfully opened its gates to the Lord of the East. Having satisfied his curiosity, the Emperor set out for Boulogne, where, under cover of the fleet which had come from the Pacific, he got ready transports to convey his army to Great Britain. But he was in need of money, and the English bought their freedom for a billion pounds.

In a year's time all the European States submitted as vassals to the domination of the Chinese Emperor, who, having left sufficient troops in Europe, returned to the East in order to organize naval expeditions against America and Australia.

For half a century Europe lay under the new Mongol yoke. In the domain of thought this epoch was remarkable for a general blending and mutual interchange of European and Eastern ideas, a repetition *en grand* of the ancient Alexandrian syncretism.

In the practical domain of life, three phenomena became characteristic in the highest degree: the large influx into Europe of Chinese and Japanese labor, and in consequence of this the violent embitterment of the social–economic question; the series of palliative attempts to solve this question, which were prolonged on the part of the governing classes; and the increasing international activity of secret social organizations which resulted in a widespread European plot to drive out the Mongols and to re–establish the independence of Europe.

This colossal plot, into which the local national governments entered so far as they were able, being under the control of the Imperial viceroys, was prepared in a masterly and succeeded in a brilliant manner. At an appointed time began the slaughter of the Mongol soldiers and the murder and expulsion of the workmen. Secret bodies of European troops were suddenly revealed in various places, and a general mobilization was carried out according to plans previously prepared.

The new Emperor, the grandson of the great Conqueror, hastened from China to Russia, but here his numberless hordes were annihilated by the all–European army. Their scattered remnants returned to the depths of Asia, and Europe became free. If the half century of subjugation to the Asiatic barbarians was the result of the disunion of the Powers, who thought only of their separate national interests, a great and glorious liberation was attained by the international organization of the united forces of all the peoples of Europe.

The long submission to the Asiatic barbarians due to the disunity of the States, which troubled themselves only about their own national interests, was now over, brought to an end by an international organization of the whole of the European population.

As a natural consequence of this fact, the old traditional organization of individual States was everywhere deprived of its former importance, and the last traces of ancient monarchical institutions gradually disappeared. Europe in the twenty–first century represented an alliance of more or less democratic nations—the United States of Europe.

The progress of material culture, somewhat interrupted by the Mongolian yoke and the war of liberation, now burst forth with a greater force. Matters of internal consciousness—questions of life and death, of the last judgment, of the world and of mankind, complicated and confused by a multitude of new physiological and psychological investigations and discoveries remained as formerly, insoluble.

Only one important negative result was made clear—the absolute fall of theoretical materialism. The representation of the universe as a system of floating atoms, and of life as the result of a mechanical agglomeration of minute alterations of matter—such a statement no longer satisfied even one thinking being. Mankind had for ever outgrown this stage of philosophical youthfulness.

But it was clear on the other hand that it had also outgrown the youthful capacity of a simple and unconscious belief. Such ideas as God, *creating* the universe *out of nothing,* were no longer taught even at elementary schools. A certain high level of ideas concerning such subjects had been evolved, and no dogmatism could risk a descent below it. And though the majority of thinking people had remained faithless, the few believers had of necessity become *thinking,* thus fulfilling the commandment of the Apostle: "Be infants in your hearts, but not in your reason."

There was at this time among the few people believing in spiritual things a remarkable man—called by many a superman—who was equally far both from infantile intellect and infantile heart. He was still young, but owing to his great genius, at the age of thirty–three he already became famous as a great thinker, writer, and politician.

Being conscious within himself of great spiritual power he had been always a convinced spiritualist, and his clear understanding always showed him the truth of that in which one must believe in—good, God, the Messiah. In these he *believed,* but he *loved only himself.* He believed in God, but, in the depths of his soul, he involuntarily and unconsciously preferred himself to Him. He believed in good, but the all–seeing eye of the Eternal knew that this man would bow down before Evil as soon as it bribed him—not by a deception of senses and base passions, not even by the bait of power, but only by his own unutterable self–love.

This self–love was neither an unconscious instinct nor an insane ambition. Apart from his exceptional genius, beauty, and nobility of character, the reserve, disinterestedness, and active sympathy with those in need, which he evinced to such a great extent, seemed abundantly to justify the immense self–love of this great spiritualist, ascetic, and philanthropist. Did he deserve blame because, being, as he was, so generously supplied with the gifts of God, he saw in them the signs of Heaven's special benevolence to him, and thought himself to be second only to God himself in his origin as the only son of God.

In a word, he avowed that he was, in truth, Christ. But this conception of his higher value showed itself in practice not in the exercise of his moral duty to God and the world, but in seizing his privilege and advantage at the expense of others, and of Christ in particular.

He had no fundamental enmity towards Jesus. He recognized His Messianic significance and merit, and he really saw in Him his own august predecessor. The moral grandeur and absolute oneness of Christ were not understood by a mind clouded by self–love. He argued thus: "Christ came before me; I appeared next, but that which appears later in time is, in reality, first. I shall come last at the end of history exactly because I am the absolute and final saviour.

The first Christ is my forerunner. His mission was to prepare and make ready for my appearance." In this sense the great man of the twenty–first century applied to himself all that was said in the Gospel about the Second Advent, proclaiming that this advent is not a return of the same Christ but a substitution of the previous Christ which is final, that is, he himself.

On this point the coming man does not yet offer much that is characteristic or original. He regards his relation to Christ in the same way as did, for instance, Mahomet, an upright man, whom it is impossible to accuse of any evil design.

The self–loving preference of himself to Christ was justified by this man with such an argument as follows: "Christ, preaching and proclaiming moral welfare, was the reformer of humanity, but I am called to be *benefactor* of humanity in part reformed, in part unreformed. I shall give to everyone all that is necessary for him. Christ as a moralist divided all people into good and bad; I shall unite them by benefits which are as much needed by good as by evil people. I shall be the true representative of that God who maketh His sun to shine upon the good and the evil, and who maketh the rain fall upon the just and upon the unjust.

Christ brought the sword; I shall bring peace. He threatened the earth with the Day of Judgment. But the last judge will be myself, and my judgment will be not only that of justice, but also that of mercy. The justice that will be meted out in my sentences will not be a retributive justice, however, but a distributive one. I shall judge every man according to his deserts , and shall give everybody what he needs."

And behold, in this beautiful frame of mind he awaits some clear, divine call for a new salvation of humanity; for some clear and striking evidence that he is the eldest and beloved firstborn Son of God. He awaits and nourishes his being with the consciousness of his superhuman beneficence and abilities—and this, as it has been said, is a man of irreproachable morality and unusual talent.

The proud and just man waits for the highest sanction in order to begin his salvation of humanity —but he waits in vain. He has passed his thirtieth year and still another three years go by. Suddenly the thought flashes into his mind and pierces to the depths of his brain with a burning shudder, "But if? if it is not I, but that other—the Galilean.

If He is not my forerunner, but the real first and last? But He must be *alive—where* is He? . . . What if He suddenly comes to me . . . here, presently? What shall I tell Him? Shall I not be compelled to kneel down before Him as the very last silly Christian, as some Russian peasant who mutters without understanding: 'Lord, Jesus Christ, forgive me, a sinful man!' I, the brilliant genius, the superman! It cannot be!"

And here, instead of his former reasoning and cold reverence to God and Christ, a sudden fear was born and grew in his heart, next followed by a burning *envy,* consuming all his being, and by an ardent hatred that takes the very breath away. "It is I, it is I, and not He! He is dead, is and will ever be! He did not—no, did not rise! His body saw corruption in the grave as that of the very last. . . ."And, his mouth foaming, he rushed in convulsive movements out of the house, through the garden, and ran along a rocky path covered by the dark gloomy night.

His rage calmed down and gave place to a despair, dry and heavy as the rocks, somber as the night. He stopped in front of a sharp precipice, from the bottom of which he could hear the faint sounds of the stream running over the stones. An unbearable anguish pressed upon his heart. Suddenly a thought flashed across his mind. "Shall I call Him? Shall I ask Him what to do?"

And in the midst of darkness he could see a pale and grief–stained image. "He pities me. . . . Oh, no, never! He did not rise! He did not! He did not! "And he leapt from the precipice. But here something firm like a column of water held him up in the air. He felt a shock as if of electricity, and some unknown force hurled him back. For a moment he became unconscious. When he came to his senses he found himself kneeling down a few paces from the brow of the precipice.

A strange figure gleaming with a dim phosphorescent light loomed up before him, and its two eyes pierced his soul with their painful penetrating glitter. He saw these two piercing eyes and heard some unfamiliar voice coming from the inside or the outside of him—he could not tell which—a dull, muffled voice, yet distinct, metallic and expressionless as from a speaker.

And the voice said to him: "Oh, my beloved son! Let all my benevolence rest on thee! Why didst not thou seek for me? Why hast thou stooped to worship that other, the bad one, and his father? I am thy god and father. And that crucified mendicant—he is a stranger both to me and to thee. I have no other son but thee. Thou art the sole, the only one begotten, the equal of myself. I love thee, and ask for nothing from thee. Thou art already beautiful, great, and mighty. Do thy work in *thine own* name, not mine. I harbor no envy of thee. I love thee. I require nothing of thee.

He whom thou regardest as a God, demanded from His Son an absolute obedience—even to death on a cross—and even there He did not help Him. I demand from thee nothing, and I will help thee. For the sake of thyself, for the sake of thine own dignity and excellency, and for the sake of my own disinterested love of thee, I will help thee! Receive thou my spirit! As before my spirit gave birth to thee in *beauty,* so now it gives birth to thee in *power.*"

With these words of the stranger, the mouth of the superman involuntarily opened, two piercing eyes came close up to his face, and he felt an icy breath which filled the whole of his being. At the same time he felt in himself such strength, vigor, lightness, and joy as he had never before experienced. At the same moment the luminous image and the two eyes suddenly disappeared, something lifted the man up in the air, and brought him down in his own garden, before the very doors of his house.

On the following day not only the visitors of the great man, but even his servants, were amazed at his inspired appearance. But they would have been still more astonished if they had been able to see with what supernatural swiftness and easiness he, having locked himself up in his own study, wrote his remarkable work under the title of "*The Open Way to Universal Peace and Prosperity.*"

The previous books and the public activity of the superman had always met with severe criticisms. though these came chiefly from men of exceptionally deep religious convictions, who for that very reason possessed no authority, and were hardly listened to when they tried to point out in everything that the "Coming Man" wrote or said, the signs of quite an exceptional and excessive self–love, and conceit, and a complete absence of true simplicity, frankness, and sincerity.

But now with his new book he brought over to his side even some of his former critics and adversaries. This book, composed after the incident at the precipice, evinced a greater power of genius than he had ever shown before.

It was a work that embraced everything and solved every problem. In it was united a noble reverence for ancient traditions and symbols, with a broad and daring radicalism in social–political demands and requirements; a boundless freedom of thought with the deepest understanding of all mysticism, unconditional individualism, with a burning zeal for the common good, the most exalted idealism in guiding principles, with the complete definiteness and vitality of practical solutions.

And all of it was united and connected with such genius and art that every thinker and every man of action, however one–sided he *may* have been, could easily view and accept the whole from his particular individual standpoint without sacrificing anything to the *truth itself,* without actually rising above his Ego, without in *reality* renouncing his one–sidedness, without correcting the inadequacy of his views and wishes, without making up their deficiencies.

This wonderful book was immediately translated into the languages of all the civilized nations, and many of the uncivilized ones as well. During the whole year thousands of papers in all parts of the world were filled with the publishers' advertisements and the eulogies of the critics.

Cheap editions, with portraits of the author, were sold in millions of copies, and the whole of the cultured world—which at that period comprised almost the whole earth—was filled with the fame of the incomparable great and only one! No one made any objections to this book—it seemed to each the revelation of entire truth. In it such full justice was done to all the past, all the present was estimated so dispassionately and broadly, and the best future was so clearly and realistically described, that everyone said: Here at last we have what we need. Here is the ideal, which is not an Utopia. Here is a scheme which is not a dream."

And the wonderful author not only impressed all, but he was agreeable to everybody, so that the word of Christ was fulfilled: "I have come in the name of the Father, and you accept me not. *Another* will come in *his own* name— him you *will* accept." For it is necessary to be *agreeable* to be accepted.

It is true, some pious people, while warmly praising the book, began to ask why Christ was not once mentioned in it; but other Christians replied, It is true some pious men, whilst praising the book whole–heartedly, had been asking why the name of Christ was never mentioned in it; but other Christians had rejoined: "So much the better.

Everything sacred has already been stained enough in the past ages to make a deeply religious author extremely careful in these matters. Then the book is imbued with the true Christian spirit of active love and all-embracing goodwill. And what more do you want?" With this everyone agreed.

Soon after the appearance of *"The Open Way,"* which made its author the most popular of all the people who had lived in the world, the international constitutional assembly of the Union of European States was to meet. This Union, founded after the series of domestic and foreign wars which were connected with the throwing off of the Mongol yoke, and which considerably changed the map of Europe, was faced with the immediate danger of a catastrophe—not between the nations, but through the internal strife between various political and social parties.

The heads of general European politics, belonging to the powerful society of Freemasons, felt the lack of a common executive authority. European unity, which had been attained with such difficulty, was threatening at any moment to fall to pieces. There was no unanimity in the Union Council or *"Comite permanent universel,"* as not all the seats were in the hands of true masons devoted to the matter.

Independent members of the committee entered into a separate agreements among themselves, and things seemed to be drifting to another war. The "initiated" then decided to establish a personal executive power endowed with some considerable authority. The principal candidate was the secret member of the Order—"the Coming Man."

He was the only man with a great world-wide fame. Being by profession a learned artilleryman, and by his source of income a rich capitalist, he was on friendly terms with many a financier and military man. In another, less enlightened time, there might have been put against him the fact of his extremely obscure origin. His mother, a lady of doubtful reputation, was very well known in both hemispheres, but too many different people had good reason to believe themselves his father. These circumstances, however, could not carry any weight with the age which was so advanced as to be actually the last one.

"The Coming Man" was almost unanimously elected president of the United States of Europe for life. And when he appeared on the platform in all the glamour of young super-human beauty and power, and with inspired eloquence expounded his universal program, the assembly was carried away by the spell of his personality, and in an outburst of enthusiasm decided, even without voting, to give him the highest honor, and to elect him Roman Emperor.

The Congress was closed amid the greatest rejoicing, and the great elector who had been chosen issued a manifesto which began thus:

> "Peoples of the earth, my peace I give to you," and ending with the words, "Peoples of the earth! The promises have been performed. An eternal, universal peace has been secured. Every attempt to destroy it will meet with invincible resistance. For, from henceforth, there is one central authority on earth, which is stronger than all other powers taken separately and together. This invincible, all-subduing authority, with all its power, belongs to me, authorized elector of Europe, the Emperor of all its forces. International law has, at last, a sanction hitherto unattained by it. From henceforth no power will dare to say 'War' when I say it is 'Peace.' Peoples of the earth, peace be to you!"

This manifesto produced the desired effect. Everywhere outside Europe, particularly in America, strong imperialistic parties were formed which forced their governments, upon various conditions, to join the United States of Europe under the supreme authority of the Roman Emperor.

There still remained a few independent tribes and little States in remote parts of Asia and Africa. The Emperor, with a small army, but one chosen from Russian, German, Polish, Hungarian and Turkish regiments, accomplished a march from Eastern Asia to Morocco, and without great bloodshed brought into subjection all who were disobedient.

He established viceroys in all the countries of both hemispheres, choosing them from among the native nobles who had been educated in European fashion and were faithful to him. In all the heathen countries the native population, greatly impressed and charmed by his personality, proclaimed him as their supreme god.

In a single year a real universal monarchy in the true and proper sense of the word was established. The germs of wars were radically destroyed. The Universal League of Peace met for the last time, and having delivered an exalted panegyric to the Great Peacemaker, dissolved itself as being no longer necessary. On the eve of the second year of his reign the World's Emperor published a new manifesto:

> "Peoples of the earth, I promised you peace and I have given it you. But peace is joyful only when coupled with prosperity. Who in peace-time is threatened with poverty has no pleasure in peace. I call, therefore, all the cold and hungry ones to come to me, and I will give them food and warmth!"

Here he announced a simple and comprehensive social reform which had already been enunciated in his book, and which then captured all the noble and sound minds. Now, owing to the concentration in his hands of the money resources of the world and of the colossal land properties, he could carry into effect that reform in accordance with the wishes of the poor and without sensibly offending the rich. Everyone began to receive in proportion to his ability, and every ability according to its labor and merit.

The new lord of the world before everything else was a kind–hearted philanthropist, and not only a philanthropist, but even a *philosopher*. He was a vegetarian himself, prohibited vivisection, and instituted a strict supervision over slaughter–houses; whilst societies for protecting animals received from him every encouragement. But what was more important than these details, the most fundamental form of equality was firmly established among mankind, the *equality of universal satiety.* This took place in the second year of his reign.

Social and economic problems had been finally settled. But if satisfaction is a question of primary importance for the hungry, the satisfied ones crave for something else. Even satiated animals usually want not only to sleep, but also to play. The more so with mankind which has always *after bread* craved for *circuses.*

The Emperor–superman understood what his mob wanted. At that time a great magician, enwrapped in a dense cloud of strange facts and wild stories, came to him in Rome from the Far East. The rumor spread amongst the neo–Buddhists credited him with a divine origin from the god of Sun Suria and some river nymph.

This magician, Apollyon by name, was a man undoubtedly talented, half Asiatic, half European, a Catholic bishop *in partibus infidelium,* who, while he was to an astonishing degree in possession of the latest results of Western science and of its technical application, also united with this the knowledge of all that is really sound and significant in the traditional mysticism of the Orient and the skill to make use of it.

The results of such a combination were astounding. Apollyon had attained, amongst other things, the skill at once, half scientific, half magical, of attracting and directing atmospheric electricity, and told the people *he brought down fire from heaven.* However, though startling the imagination of the crowd by various unheard of phenomena, for some time he did not abuse his power for any special selfish ends.

It was this man who came to the great Emperor, saluted him as the true son of God, declared that he had discovered in the secret books of the East certain unmistakable prophecies pointing to the Emperor as the last saviour and judge of the Universe, and offered him his services and all his art.

The Emperor, completely charmed by the man, accepted him as a gift from above, decorated him with all kinds of gorgeous titles and made him his constant companion. So the nations of the world, after they had received from their lord universal peace and universal abolition of hunger, were now given the possibility of never-ending enjoyment of most diverse and extraordinary miracles. Thus came to end the third year of the reign of the superman.

After the happy solution of political and social problems, the religious question was brought to the front. This was raised by the Emperor himself, and in the first place in its application to Christianity. At the time the position of Christianity was as follows: Its followers had greatly diminished in numbers and barely included forty-five million men in the whole world; but morally it made a marked progress, and gained in quality what it lost in numbers.

Men who were not bound up with Christianity by any spiritual tie were no longer recorded amongst the Christians. Various Christian persuasions fairly equally diminished in their numbers, so that the proportional relationship amongst them was maintained almost unchanged.

As to mutual feelings, hostility did not entirely give place to amity, but considerably softened down, and points of disagreement lost much of their former acuteness. The Papacy had been long before expelled from Rome, and after long wanderings had found refuge in St. Petersburg on condition that it refrained from propaganda there, and in the country. In Russia it soon became greatly simplified. Leaving practically unchanged the number of its colleges and offices, it was obliged to infuse into their work a more fervent spirit, and also to reduce to a minimum its magnificent ritual and ceremonial. Many strange and seductive customs, though not formally abolished, fell of themselves into disuse.

In all the other countries, particularly in North America, the Catholic priesthood still had a good, many representatives, possessed of strong will, inexhaustible energy and independent character, who welded together the Catholic Church into a closer unity than it had ever been before, and who preserved for it its international, cosmopolitan importance.

As to Protestantism, which was still led by Germany, especially since the union of the greater part of the Anglican church with the Catholic one—this had freed itself from its extreme negative tendencies, the followers of which openly went over to the camp of religious apathy and unbelief.

The Evangelical church now contained only the sincerely religious, headed by men who combined a vast learning with a deep religious feeling, and an ever-growing desire to bring to life again in their own persons the living spirit of the true ancient Christianity.

Russian orthodoxy, after political events had altered the official position of the Church, lost many millions of its sham nominal members; but it won the joy of unification with the best part of the "Old Believers," and even many of the positively religious sectarians. This renovated Church, though not increasing in numbers, began to grow in strength of spirit, which it particularly revealed in its struggle with the numerous sects, sects not entirely devoid of the demoniacal and satanic element, which had found root among the people and in society.

During the first two years of the new reign, all Christians, frightened at, and weary of, the number of preceding revolutions and wars, looked upon their new lord and his peaceful reforms partly with a benevolent expectation, and partly with an unreserved, sympathetic, and even a fervent enthusiasm. But in the third year, after the great magician had made his appearance, serious fears and antipathy began to grow in the minds of many an orthodox Catholic and Protestant.

The Gospel and Apostolic texts speaking of the Prince of this Age and of Anti-Christ were now read more carefully and led to lively comments. The Emperor soon perceived from certain signs that a storm was brewing, and resolved to bring the matter to a head without any further delay. In the beginning of the fourth year of his reign he published a manifesto to all his true Christians, without distinction of churches, inviting them to elect or appoint authoritative representatives for the World's Congress to be held under his presidency. At that time the imperial residence was transferred from Rome to Jerusalem.

Palestine was then an autonomous State inhabited and governed principally by Jews. Jerusalem was a free and now an imperial city. The Christian shrines remained unmolested, but over the whole of the large platform of Haram-esh-Sheriff, extending from Birket-Israin and the barracks right to the mosque of El-Ax and the "Solomon's Stables," there was erected an immense building, which incorporated in itself, besides the two small ancient mosques, a huge "Imperial" temple for the unification of all cults, and two luxurious imperial palaces, with libraries, museums, and special apartments for magic experiments and exercises.

In this half-temple, half-palace, the general council was to be opened on the 14th of September. Since the Evangelical religion has no priesthood in the true sense, the Catholic and Orthodox hierarchy, in compliance with the express wish of the Emperor, and in order that a greater uniformity of representation should obtain, decided to admit to the proceedings of the congress a certain number of lay members.

Once, however, these were admitted, it seemed impossible to exclude from the congress the clergy, both of the monastic and secular order. In this way the total number of members at the congress exceeded three thousand, whilst about half a million Christian pilgrims flooded Jerusalem and all Palestine.

Amongst the members present three men were particularly conspicuous. The first was Pope Peter II., who in true right led the Catholic part of the congress. His predecessor died on the way to the congress, and a conclave met in Damascus, which unanimously elected Cardinal Simone Barionini, who took the name of Peter. He came of plebeian stock, from the province of Naples, and became famous as a preacher of the Carmelite Order, having earned great successes in fighting a certain Satanic sect which was spreading in St. Petersburg and its environments, and seducing not only the Orthodox, but the Catholic men as well.

Raised to the archbishopric of Mogilev and then cardinal, he was early marked out for the tiara. He was a man of fifty, of middle stature and strongly built, had a red face, a crooked nose, and thick eyebrows. He had an impulsive and ardent temperament, spoke with fervor and with sweeping gesticulations, and enthused more than convinced his audience.

The new Pope had no trust in the Emperor, and looked at him with a disapproving eye, particularly since the deceased Pope, yielding to the Emperor's pressure, made a cardinal of the Imperial Chancellor and great magician of the world, the exotic Bishop Apollonius, whom Peter regarded as a doubtful Catholic and a doubtless fraud.

The actual, though unofficial, leader of the Orthodox was the Starets[26] John, extremely well known among the Russian people. Officially he was considered a bishop "in retirement," but he did not live in any monastery, being always engaged in travelling all over the world.

Many legendary stories were circulated about him. Some people believed that he was Feodor. Kusmich, that is, Emperor Alexander I., who had died three centuries back and was now raised to life. Others went further and maintained that he was the true Starets John, that is, John the Apostle, who had never died and openly reappeared in the later times.

---

[26] Starets, Russian: ста́рец, or Elder in English. Ed.

He himself said nothing about his origin and younger days. Now he was a very old but vigorous man, with white hair and beard tinged with a yellowish and even greenish color, tall in stature, and thin in the body, but with full and slightly rosy cheeks, vivid sparkling eyes and a tender and kind expression in his face and speech. He was always dressed in a white cassock and mantle.

At the head of the evangelical members of the congress was the most learned German theologian, Professor Ernst Pauli. He was a short, wizened, little old man, with a huge forehead, sharp nose, and cleanly–shaven chin. His eyes were distinguished by their peculiarly ferocious and yet at one and the same time kindly gaze. He incessantly rubbed his hands, shook his head, sternly knitted his brows and pursed up his lips; whilst with eyes all flashing he sternly ejaculated: "So! Nun! Ja! So also!" His dress bore all the appearance of solemnity—a white tie and long pastoral frock–coat decorated with signs of his orders.

The opening of the congress was very imposing. Two–thirds of the immense temple, devoted to the "unification of all the cults," were covered with benches and other sitting accommodation for members of the congress. The remaining third was taken by the high platform, on which were placed the Emperor's throne, another a little below it intended for the great magician—who was also the cardinal–imperial chancellor; and behind them rows of armchairs for the ministers, courtiers, and State officials, whilst along the side there were the still longer rows of armchairs, the intended occupants of which remained undisclosed.

In the choir was an orchestra and, on a neighboring platform, two regiments of the guards were drawn up and a battery for triumphant salvos. The members of the council had already celebrated religious services in their various churches, and the opening of the council was to be entirely secular. When the Emperor, accompanied by the great magician and his suite, made his entrance, the band began to play the "March of Unified Mankind," which was the international hymn of the Empire, and all the members rose to their feet, and waving their hats, gave three enthusiastic cheers: "Vivat! Hurrah! Hoch!"

The Emperor, standing by the throne and stretching forward his hand with the air of majestic benevolence, said in a sonorous and pleasing voice: "Christians of all sects! My beloved subjects and brothers! From the beginning of my reign, which the Most High blessed with such wonderful and glorious deeds, I have never had any cause to be dissatisfied with you. You have always performed your duties true to your faith and conscience. But this is not sufficient for me.

My sincere love to you, my beloved brothers, thirsts for reciprocation. I wish you to recognize me your true leader in every enterprise undertaken for the well–being of mankind, not merely out of your sense of duty to me, but mainly out of your heartfelt love for me. So now, besides what I generally do for all, I am about to show you my special benevolence. Christians! tell me what is dearer to you than aught else in Christianity, so that I may in this matter direct your efforts. Christians! what can I do to make you happy?

What shall I give you, not as my subjects, but as fellow–believers, as my brethren. Christians! tell me what is dearer to you than anything else in Christianity, so that I may in this matter direct your efforts." He stopped for a time, waiting for an answer. The hall was filled with reverberating muffled sounds. The members of the congress were consulting each other. Pope Peter, with fervent gesticulations, was explaining something to his followers. Professor Pauli was shaking his head and ferociously smacking with his lips. Starets John bending over an Eastern bishop and a Capuchin quietly tried to impress something upon them.

After he had waited a few minutes, the Emperor again addressed the congress in the same kind tone, in which, however, there could be sounded a scarcely perceptible note of irony: "My kind Christians," said he, "I understand how difficult it is for you to give me a direct answer. I will help you also in this. From time immemorial, unfortunately, you have been broken up into various confessions and sects, so that you perhaps have scarcely one common object of desire.

But if you cannot agree amongst yourselves, I hope I shall be able to show agreement with you all by bestowing upon all your sections the same love and the same readiness to satisfy the *true* desire of each one of them. Kind Christians! I know that to many, and not the last ones amongst you, the most precious thing in Christianity is the *spiritual authority* with which it endows its legal representatives—of course, not for their personal benefit, but for the common good, since on this authority the right spiritual order and moral discipline so necessary for everybody, firmly rest.

Kind brothers—Catholic! How well do I understand your view, and how much would I like to base my imperial power on the authority of your spiritual chief! Lest you should think that this is a mere flattery and empty phrases we most solemnly declare: by virtue of our autocratic power the Supreme Bishop of all the Catholics, the Pope of Rome, is henceforth restored to his throne in Rome, with all the former rights and privileges belonging to this title and chair, given at any time by our predecessors, from Constantine the Great onwards.

For this, brothers–Catholic, I wish to receive from you only your inner heart–felt recognition of myself as your sole protector and patron. Whoever of those present here does recognize me as such in his heart and conscience, let him come up here to this side!" Here he pointed to the empty seats on the platform.

And instantly, nearly all the princes of the Catholic Church, cardinals and bishops, the greater part of the laymen and over a half of the monks, shouting in exultation: "Gratias agimus! Domine! Salvum fac magnum imperatorem!" rose to the platform and, humbly bowing their heads to the Emperor, took their seats.

Below, however, in the middle of the hall, straight and immovable, like a marble statue, sat in his seat Pope Peter II. All those who had surrounded him were now on the platform. But the diminished crowd of monks and laymen who remained below moved nearer and closed in a dense crowd around him. And one could hear the subdued mutter issuing from them: "Non praevalebunt, non praevalebunt portae inferni."

With a startled look cast at the immovable Pope, the Emperor again raised his voice: "Kind brothers! I know that there are amongst you many for whom the most precious thing in Christianity is its *sacred tradition*— the old symbols, the old hymns and prayers, the icons and the old ritual. Indeed, what can be more precious for a religious soul?

Know, then, my beloved ones, that today I have signed the decree and have set aside vast sums of money for the establishment in our glorious Empire city, Constantinople, of a world's museum of Christian archaeology, with the object of collecting, studying, and saving all the monuments of church antiquity, more particularly of the Eastern one; and I ask you to select from your midst a committee for working out with me the measures which are to be carried out, so that the modern life, morals, and customs may be organized as nearly as possible in accordance with the traditions and institutions of the Holy Orthodox Church.

My orthodox brothers! Those of you who view with favor this will of mine, who can in their inner consciousness call me their true leader and lord—let those come up here." Here the greater part of the hierarchs of the East and North, and more than a half of the orthodox clergymen, monks, and laymen, rose with joyful exclamation to the platform, casting suspicious eyes at the Catholics, who were already proudly occupying their seats.

But Starets John remained in his place, and sighed loudly. And when the crowd round him became greatly thinned, he left his bench and went over to Pope Peter and his group. He was followed by the other orthodox members who did not go to the platform.

Then the Emperor spoke again: "I am aware, kind Christians, that there are amongst you also such who place the greatest value upon the personal confidence in truth and the free examination of the Scriptures. How I view this, there is no need for me to enlarge upon at the moment. You are perhaps aware that even in my youth I wrote a big book on the Higher Criticism, which at that time excited much comment and laid the foundation of my popularity.

In memory of this, I presume, the University of Tubingen only the other day requested me to accept the degree of a Doctor of Theology *honoris causa*. I have replied that I accept it with pleasure and gratitude. And today, simultaneously with the decree of the Museum of Christian Archaeology, I signed another decree establishing a world's institute for free examination of the Scriptures from all sides and in all directions, and for study of all subsidiary sciences, to which an annual sum of one and a half million marks is granted.

I call those of you who look with sincere favor at this my act of goodwill, and are able in their true feeling to recognize me their sovereign leader, to come up here to the new Doctor of Theology." A strange but hardly perceptible smile changed the beautiful mouth of the great man when he concluded this speech. More than half of the learned theologians were moving to the platforms, though somewhat slowly and hesitatingly.

Everybody looked at Professor Pauli, who seemed to be rooted to his seat. He dropped his head, bent down and shrank. The learned theologians who had already managed to get on the platform seemed to feel very awkward, and one of them even suddenly dropped his hand in renunciation, and, having jumped right down past the stairs, ran hobbling to Professor Pauli and the members who remained with him.

At this the Professor raised his head, got up on his feet as if without a definite object in view, and then walked past the empty benches, accompanied by his co–religionists who withstood the temptation, and took his seat near Starets John and Pope Peter with their followers.

The greater part of the members, including nearly all the hierarchs of the East and West, were now on the platform. Below there remained only the three groups of members now more closely brought together, who clung around to Starets John, Pope Peter, and Professor Pauli.

In a grieved voice the Emperor addressed them: "What else can I do for you, you strange people? What do you want from me? I cannot understand. Tell me yourselves, you Christians, deserted by the majority of your brothers and leaders, condemned by popular sentiment: what is it that you value most in Christianity?"

At this Starets John rose up like a white taper, and said in a quiet voice: "Great sovereign! The thing we value most in Christianity is Christ Himself—He in His person. All the rest cometh from Him, for we know that in Him dwelleth bodily the whole fullness of Divinity. But we are ready, sire, to accept any gift from you as well, if only we recognize the holy hand of Christ in your generosity.

Our candid answer to your question, what you can do for us, is this: Here, now and before us, name the name of Jesus Christ, the Son of God, who came in the flesh, rose, and is coming again—name His name, and we will accept you with love as the true forerunner of His second glorious coming." He finished his speech and fixed his eyes on the face of the Emperor.

A terrible change had come over it. A hellish storm was raging within him, like the one he experienced on that fateful night. He had entirely lost his mental balance, and was concentrating all his thoughts on preserving control over his appearance, so that he should not betray himself before the time.

He was making superhuman efforts not to throw himself, yelling wildly, on Starets John and begin tearing him with his teeth. Suddenly he heard a familiar, unearthly voice: "Keep silent and fear nothing!" He remained silent. Only his face, livid like death, looked distorted and his eyes flashed.

In the meantime, while Starets John was still making his speech, the great magician, wrapped in his ample tri–colored mantle, which concealed nearly the whole of his cardinal purple, could be noticed to be busy doing something underneath it. His eyes were fixed and flashing, and his lips slightly moving. It could be seen through the open windows of the temple that an immense black cloud was covering the sky, and soon a complete darkness set in.

Starets John, startled and frightened, stared at the face of the silent Emperor, when he suddenly sprang back, and turning to his followers shouted in a stifled voice: "My dearest ones, it is Anti–Christ!" At this moment, followed by a deafening thunderclap, a great thunderbolt flashed into the temple and struck Starets John. Everyone was stupefied for a second, and when the deafened Christians came to their senses, Starets John was seen lying dead on the floor.

The Emperor, pale but calm, spoke to the assembly: "You have witnessed the judgment of God. I had no wish to take any man's life, but thus my Heavenly Father avenges His beloved son. It is finished. Who will oppose the will of the Most High? Secretaries, write down: The ecumenical Council of All Christians, after an insensate opponent of the

Divine Majesty had been struck by fire from heaven, recognized unanimously the sovereign Emperor of Rome and all the Universe its supreme leader and lord."

Suddenly a word, loudly distinct, passed throughout the temple: "Contradicatur!" Pope Peter II rose, and with face empurpled and his body trembling with indignation, lifted up his stick in the direction of the Emperor. "Our only Lord," shouted he, "is Jesus Christ, the Son of the living God! And who, thou art, thou heardest just now. Away! thou Cain, thou murderer! Get thee gone, thou incarnation of the Devil!

By the authority of Christ, I, the servant of God's servants, for ever expel thee, thou foul dog, from the precincts of God, and cast thee out to thy father Satan! Anathema! Anathema! Anathema! "While he was so speaking, the great magician was moving restlessly under his mantle, and louder than the last "Anathema!" the thunder rumbled, and the last Pope fell lifeless on the floor.

"So die all my enemies by the arm of my Father!" said the Emperor. "Pereant, pereant!" exclaimed the trembling princes of the Church. He turned and, leaning upon the shoulder of the great magician, accompanied by all the throng, went out slowly by a door behind the dais.

There remained in the temple only the corpses and a little knot of Christians half–dead from fear. The only person who did not lose control over himself was Professor Pauli. The general horror seemed to have raised in him all the powers of his spirit. He even changed in appearance; his countenance became noble and inspired. With determined steps he walked up on to the platform, took one of the seats previously occupied by some State official, and began to write on a sheet of paper. When he had finished he got up and read out in a loud voice:

"In the glory of our only saviour, Jesus Christ! The Ecumenical Council of our Lord's churches, which met at Jerusalem after our most blessed brother John, the representative of Christianity of the East, had exposed the arch–deceiver and the enemy of God as the true Anti–Christ, foretold in the word of God, and after our most blessed father Peter, the representative of Christianity of the West, had lawfully and justly expelled him for ever from the Church of God.

Now in the face of the corpses of these two witnesses of Christ, murdered for the truth, the Council resolves: To cease any communion with the excommunicated one and with his foul crowd, and to go to the desert and to wait for the inevitable coming of our true Lord, Jesus Christ." The crowd was seized with enthusiasm, and loud exclamations could be heard on all sides. "Adveniat! Adveniat cito! Komm, Herr Jesu, komm! Come, Lord Jesus Christ! "

Professor Pauli wrote again and read: "Accepting unanimously this first and last deed of the last ecumenical Council, we sign our names "— and here he invited those present to do so. All hurried to the platform and signed their names. And last in the list stood in big Gothic characters the signature: "Duorum defunctorum testium locum tenens Ernst Pauli."

"Now let us go with our ark of the last covenant," said he, pointing to the two deceased. The corpses were put on stretchers. Slowly, singing Latin, German and Church–Slavonic hymns, the Christians walked to the gate leading out from Haram–esh–Sheriff. Here the procession was stopped by one of the Emperor's officials, who was accompanied by a squad of the Guards. The soldiers remained at the entrance whilst the official read:

"By order of his Divine Majesty. For the enlightenment of the Christian people and for its safety from wicked men spreading unrest and seducing the people, we deem necessary to resolve that the corpses of the two agitators, killed by the heavenly fire, be publicly exhibited in the street of the Christians (Haret–en–Nasara), at the entrance into the principal temple of this religion, called the Temple of our Lord's Sepulchre, also that of the Resurrection, so that everybody may convince himself that they are really dead.

Their obstinate followers, who wrathfully reject all our benefits and insanely shut their eyes to the patent signs of Deity itself—are by our mercy and presentations before our Heavenly Father, relieved from a much–deserved death by the heavenly fire, and are left at their free will with the sole prohibition, necessary for the common good, of living in towns and other places of residence, lest they disturb and tempt innocent, simple–minded folk with their malicious fancies." When he had finished reading, eight soldiers, at the sign of the officer, came up with stretchers to the bodies.

"Let the written word be fulfilled," said Professor Pauli. And the Christians who were holding the stretchers silently passed them to the soldiers, who went away with them through the north–western gate, whilst the Christians, having gone out through the north–eastern gate, hurriedly walked from the city past the Mount of Olives to Jericho, along the road which had previously been cleared of other people by the gendarmes and two cavalry regiments. It was decided to wait a few days on the desert hills near Jericho.

Next morning, friendly Christian pilgrims came from Jerusalem and told what had been going on in Sion. After the dinner at the Court all the members of the congress were invited to a vast throne hall (near the supposed site of Solomon's throne), and the Emperor, addressing the representatives of the Catholic hierarchy, told them that the well-being of their Church clearly demanded from them the immediate election of a worthy successor to the apostate Peter.

That in the circumstances of the time the election must needs be a summary one, that his the Emperor's presence as that of the leader and representative of the whole Christian world, would amply make up for the inevitable omissions in the ritual, and that he on behalf of all the Christians suggested that the Sacred College elect his beloved friend and brother Apollonius, so that their close friendship could firmly and indissolubly unite Church and State for their mutual benefit.

The Sacred College retired to a separate room for a conclave, and in an hour and a half it returned with its new Pope Apollonius. In the meantime, while the election was being carried out, the Emperor was meekly, sagaciously, and eloquently persuading the Orthodox and Evangelical representatives, in view of the new great era in Christian history, to put an end to their old dissensions, giving his word that Apollonius would be able to abolish all the abuses of the Papal authority known to history.

Persuaded by this speech, the Orthodox and Protestant representatives drafted a deed of the unification of all the churches, and when Apollonius with the cardinals appeared in the hall, met by shouts of joy from all those present, a Greek bishop and an evangelical pastor presented to him their document. "Accipio et approbo et lmtificatur cor meum," said Apollonius, signing it. "I am as much a true Orthodox and a Protestant as I am a true Catholic," added he, and exchanged friendly kisses with the Greek and the German.

Then he came up to the Emperor, who embraced him and long field him in his arms. At this time tongues of flame began to dart about in the palace and the temple. They grew and became transformed into luminous shapes of strange beings, and flowers never seen before came down from above, filling the air with unknown aroma. Enchanting sounds of music, stirring the very depths of the soul, produced by unfamiliar instruments, were heard, while angelic voices of unseen singers sang the glory of the new lords of heaven and earth.

Suddenly a terrific subterranean noise was heard in the north-western corner of the palace under "Kubbet-el-Aruah," that is "the dome of souls," where, according to the Moslem belief, the entrance to the hell was hidden. When the assembly invited by the Emperor went to that end all could clearly hear innumerable voices, thin and penetrating—either childish or devilish—which were exclaiming: "The time has come, do let us out, dear saviours, dear saviours!

"But when Apollonius, kneeling on the ground, shouted something down in an unknown language three times, the voices died down and the subterranean noise subsided. Meanwhile a vast crowd of people surrounded Haram–esh–Sheriff on all sides. Darkness set in and the Emperor, with the new Pope, came out upon the eastern terrace—the signal for a storm of rejoicings.

The Emperor bowed affably to the people around, whilst Apollonius, taking from the huge baskets brought up by the cardinal–deacons, incessantly threw into the air, making them burn by mere touch of his hand, magnificent fireworks, rockets, and fountains, that now glimmered like phosphorescent pearls, and now sparkled with all the tints of a rainbow. On reaching the ground all the sparkles transformed into numberless variously colored sheets containing complete and absolute indulgences of all sins—past, present, and future.[27]

The popular exultation overflowed all limits. True, there were some who stated that they had seen with their own eyes the indulgences turn into hideous frogs and snakes. But the vast majority of the people were pleased immensely, and the popular festivities continued a few days longer. The prodigies of the new Pope now surpassed all imagination, so that it would be a hopeless task even to attempt a description of them. In the meantime among the desert hills of Jericho the Christians were devoting themselves to fasting and prayers.

On the night of the fourth day Professor Pauli, with nine comrades riding on asses and having a cart with them, succeeded in getting inside Jerusalem and passing through side–streets by Haram–esh–Sheriff to Haret–en–Nasara, came to the entrance to the Temple of Resurrection, in front of which, on the pavement, the bodies of Pope Peter and Starets John were lying.

The street was deserted at that time of night, as all the people had gone to Hasam–esh–Sheriff. The sentries were fast asleep. The party that came for the bodies found them quite untouched by decomposition, not even stiff or heavy. They put them on the stretchers covered with the cloaks they had brought with them, and by the same circuitous road went back to their followers. They had hardly lowered the stretchers to the ground when suddenly the spirit of fife could be seen re–entering the deceased bodies.

---

[27] With reference to the above, see Preface.—Author.

They moved slightly as if they were trying to throw off the cloaks in which they were wrapped. With shouts of joy everyone lent them aid, and soon both the revived men rose to their feet safe and sound. Then said Starets John: "Ah, my dear ones, we have not parted after all! I will tell you this: it is time that we carry out the last prayer of Christ about His disciples—that they should be all one, even as He Himself is one with the Father. For this unity in Christ let us honor our beloved brother Peter. Let him at last pasture the flocks of Christ. There it is, brother!" And he put his arms round Peter.

Here Professor Pauli came nearer. "Tu es Petrus!" said he to the Pope, *"jetzt ist es ja grundlich erwiesen and ausser jedem Zweifel gesetzt."*[28] And he shook Peter's hand firmly with his own right hand, whilst his left hand he stretched out to John, saying: *"So also Väterchen nun sind wir ja Eins in Christo."*[29]

In this manner the unification of churches took place in the midst of a dark night, on a high and deserted spot. But the night darkness was suddenly illuminated with brilliant light and a great sign appeared in the heavens; it was—a woman, clothed in the sun with the moon beneath her feet, and a wreath of twelve stars on her head. The apparition remained immovable for some time, and then began slowly to move in a southerly direction. Pope Peter raised his stick and exclaimed: "Here is our sign! Let us follow it! "And he walked after the apparition, accompanied by both old men and the whole crowd of the Christians, to God's mountain, to Sinai. . . ."

(Here the reader stopped.)

LADY.—Why don't you continue?

MR. Z.— The manuscript stops here. Father Pansophius could not finish his story. He told me when he was already ill that he thought of completing it "as soon as I get better," he said. But he did not get better, and the end of his story is buried with him in the graveyard of the Danilov Monastery.

LADY.—But you remember what he told you,! don't you? Please tell us.

MR. Z.— I remember it only in the main outlines. After the spiritual leaders and representatives of Christianity withdrew to the Arabian desert, where crowds of faithful zealots of truth flocked to them from all countries, the new Pope was able, without any obstacle, to pervert by his

---

[28] This has now been thoroughly proved and placed beyond a shadow of a doubt. Ed.

[29] Now then, dear Father, we are *one* in Christ. Ed.

134

wonders and prodigies all the superficial Christians who had not been disillusioned by Antichrist, and who remained with him.

He declared that by the power of his keys he could open the gates to other worlds. Communion of the living with the dead, and also of men with demons, became a matter of everyday occurrence, and new unheard-of forms of mystic lust and demonology began to spread amongst the people. However, the Emperor scarcely began to feel himself firmly established on religious grounds, and, yielding to the persistent suggestions of the seductive voice of the "father," had hardly declared himself the sole true incarnation of the supreme Deity of the Universe, when a new trouble came upon him from a side from which nobody expected it: the Jews rose against him.

This nation, which at that time reached thirty millions, was not altogether unfamiliar with the paving of the way for the world's successes of the superman. When this latter transferred his residence to Jerusalem, secretly spreading amongst the Jews the rumor that his main object was to bring about a domination of Israel over the whole of the world, the Jews proclaimed him as their Messiah, and their exultation and devotion to him knew no bounds.

And now they suddenly rose, full of wrath and thirsting for vengeance. This turn of events, doubtless foretold both in the Gospel and in the church tradition, was pictured by Father Pansophius, perhaps, with too great a simplicity and realism. You see, the Jews, who regarded the Emperor a true and perfect Israelite by blood, unexpectedly discovered that he was not even circumcised.

The same day all Jerusalem, and next day all Palestine, were up in arms against him. The boundless and fervent devotion to the saviour of Israel, the promised Messiah, gave place to as boundless and as fervent a hatred of the wily deceiver, the impudent impostor. The whole of the Jewish nation rose as one man, and its enemies were surprised to see that the soul of Israel at bottom lived not by calculations and aspirations of Mammon but by the power of an all-absorbing sentiment—the hope and strength of its eternal faith in the Messiah.

The Emperor, taken by surprise at the sudden outburst, lost all self-control, and issued a decree sentencing to death all the insubordinate Jews and Christians. Many thousands and tens of thousands who could not arm themselves in time were ruthlessly massacred. But an army of Jews, a million strong, soon took Jerusalem, and locked up Anti-Christ in Haram-esh-Sheriff. His only support was a portion of the Guards, who were not strong enough to overwhelm the masses of the enemy.

Assisted by the magic art of his Pope, the Emperor succeeded in finding his way through the besieging army, and soon appeared again in Syria at the head of an innumerable army of pagans. The Jews advanced to meet him, with little chance of gaining success. But no sooner had the outposts of the armies come in contact with each other than a terrific earthquake broke out.

The crater of a tremendous volcano rose from the bottom of the Dead Sea, on the shores of which the Emperor's army had built their camp, and fiery streams mingling in a single lake of fire swallowed up the Emperor, all his innumerable troops, and his constant companion, Pope Apollonius, to whom even his magic art proved of no help. At the same time the Jews were running to Jerusalem in fear and horror, praying to the God of Israel to deliver them from peril.

When the Holy City was already in sight, a great lightning cut the sky open from east to west, and they saw Christ descending to them clad in kingly apparel, and with the wounds from the nails on His outstretched hands. At the same time a crowd of Christians, led by Peter, John, and Paul, were moving from Sinai to Sion, and other crowds, all seized with enthusiasm, came flocking from all sides. These were all the Jews and Christians executed by the Anti–Christ. They rose to life, and reigned with Christ for a thousand years.

At this point Father Pansophius thought to finish his story, which was to picture not the final catastrophe of the Universe, but only the conclusion of our historical process. This end is the coming, the glorification, and the destruction of Anti–Christ.

POLITICIAN.—And do you think that this conclusion is so near?

MR. Z.— Well, there will still be a good deal of rattling and bustling on the stage, but the drama has been all written long ago, and neither the audience nor the actors are allowed to alter anything in it.

LADY.—What is, however, the ultimate meaning of this drama? I cannot understand, moreover, why your Anti–Christ hates God so much whilst in essence he is really kind and not wicked at all.

MR. Z.— No. Not "in essence." That is just the point. That is the whole matter. I take back my previous words that "you cannot explain Antichrist by proverbs alone." In point of fact, he is completely explained by a single and extremely simple proverb: "All that glitters is not gold." Of sham glitter he indeed has more than enough; but of the essential force — nothing.

GENERAL.— I beg to call your attention to yet another thing. But you notice, too, upon what the curtain falls in this historical drama—upon war—the meeting of two armies. So the end of our discussion comes again back to its beginning. How do you like it, Prince? Good heavens, but where is the Prince?

POLITICIAN.—Didn't you see, then? He quietly left us at that pathetic scene when Starets John drove the Anti-Christ into a corner. I did not want to interrupt the reading at that time, and afterwards I forgot.

GENERAL—He has ran away, I swear it, and that's the second time. He mastered himself the first time and came back. But this last was too much for him: he could not stand it for anything. Oh, dear me! dear me!

THE END

APPENDIX

THE ANTICHRIST UNMASKED
BY VLADIMIR SOLOVIEV

REASONS FOR ENTHUSIASM

We have been delighted to rediscover, under our Abbé's guidance, the doctrine of one of the greatest modern Russian geniuses, whose sublime, lucid and receptive mind has amazed many of our friends. Vladimir Soloviev (1853– 1900) was more than a philosopher in the classical sense of the term. This "lover of wisdom" was also an authentic prophet, whose transparent soul was the mirror in which a mysterious and luminous *Sophia* was reflected.

<< Very tall, thin, of ancient appearance, a "living relic" according to his friends, he possessed the head of a prophet from the Old Testament and remarkable eyes with a far–off look in them as though he were focusing on something in the beyond. He possessed the gift of clairvoyance and was often aware of what was going on far away from him. People used to come to him for advice : with his eyes closed and in prayer, he would give his reply. His long hair, falling on his shoulders, made him look like an icon. Children used to say : "It is the Good God."

<< Of an infectious good humor and an inexhaustible charity, he was frequently unable to go out because he had given all his clothes away to the poor. He was a true pilgrim, having neither a permanent dwelling nor any material worries. >> (Paul Evdokimov, *Christ in Russian thought*, Paris, 1970, p. 105)

We find ourselves in an astonishing communion of thought with him, particularly with his theology of history, which is wholly orientated towards the ultimate Catholic world civilization.

<< Soloviev, and we ourselves therefore >>, explains our Abbé, << possess a lofty ideal, a mystical rather than a moralizing ideal : it involves the total and universal union – "each man and all men" – of creation to its Creator, in grace and love. Such is *Theandry*. We know through which institutions it will come, since they exist already and enjoy the divine promise of indefectible assistance : the Churches of East and West, the Churches of John, Peter and Paul, and the Christendom of the Nations under the guidance of our " gentle Christ on earth ", the Pope of Rome : such is *Theocracy*, the supreme hope. >> (English CRC n° 115, p. 18)

In the designs of God, Russia has been allotted a unique vocation, a vocation which she will fulfill when her leader recognizes himself as a << ***son of the Church*** >>, the head of a political body itself irrigated by grace and belonging to the Mystical Body of Christ. It is only then that the *Russian Idea* will be realized :

<< The profoundly religious and monarchical character of the Russian people, certain prophetic facts in their past, the enormous compact mass of their Empire, the latent strength of their national spirit in contrast to the poverty and emptiness of their current existence, all this seems to indicate that the historical destiny of Russia is to provide the universal Church with the political power necessary for her to revitalise Europe and the world. >> (*Russia and the Church Universal*, p. 147)

Soloviev's mystical nationalism is closely akin – and how marvelous this is! – to our own which is totally permeated by Christian virtue and sparkles with a divine beauty. Pope Saint Pius X gave a most beautiful definition of it in his Letter of 6 January 1907 : << "*France, a predestined nation, is an **integral part of the Church**.*" That does not rule out, adds our Abbé, the possibility of other nations enjoying comparable privileges. On the contrary, it is understood that all nations are called, that all peoples are themselves invited to follow the example of their elder sister France, as properly constituted political bodies, and to share politically in the mystical life of the Church, benefiting from the same divine animation, the same influence of grace on their whole national being, each according to its own political character – a character which in France, throughout the centuries of her greatness and holiness, was both royal and sacral. >> (French CRC n° 195, *The Nation, the fundamental political reality*, p. 13)

BUT FIRST MUST COME THE ANTICHRIST !

Soloviev's theocratic politics, like the ecumenical projects he formed with Mgr Strossmayer and Canon Racki, Zagreb, unfortunately remained a dead letter. After having read *The Russian Idea*, Leo XIII declared : << *It is a beautiful idea, but in the absence of a miracle, the thing is impossible.* >> All the more impossible in that this liberal Pope was pursuing a quite different policy!

Misunderstood by Rome and by the Jesuits who were initially interested in his writings, Soloviev was violently criticized by his co-religionists on his return to Russia. His confessor even refused him sacramental absolution in 1891, telling him : << Make your confession to your own Catholic priests! >> Soloviev suffered much from such contradictions and narrow-mindedness, but he would not relinquish his views on the Church and the Christendom of the future. << Soloviev was too great a mind to be discouraged or to modify his ideas in accordance with the ups and downs of worldly success. It remains true, however, that these bitter experiences gave him a better understanding of how Evil was at work in the world, throwing up formidable obstacles to Theocracy and even going so far as to erect ***a kind of caricature theocracy wherein he saw and denounced the power of the Antichrist, the Prince of this world foretold in the Scriptures.*** >> (English CRC n₀ 115, October 1979, p. 15)

Throughout his life, he had never ceased thinking of these forces of Evil ranged against those of the Good, against God and His Christ : << In my childhood, at moments when feelings of religious elation made me desire to become a monk, I started inflicting severe physical penances on myself, expecting as I did the imminent advent of the Antichrist and desiring to die a martyr for the Faith. >> (quoted by his nephew in his *Life of Soloviev*, p. 48)

To believe Mgr Rupp, he also seems to have personally experienced the physical presence of the devil (cf. *The Ecclesial Message of Soloviev*, p. 350). Soloviev knew that the divine *Sophia* and her implacable adversary, the accursed Serpent, were engaged in a mighty combat. He threw himself into this combat with all the strength of his immense genius and, with eagle vision, was able to detect the telltale signs of the coming of the Antichrist, in whom the mystery of iniquity would be revealed.

« SOMEONE IS COMING... »

The famine of 1891 which claimed numerous victims in several Russian provinces, the growing threat of the yellow peril, Japan and China merged together in a devastating Pan–Mongolism, and the increasing mental disorder of Russian society at the end of the nineteenth century, all appeared to Soloviev as ominous signs. Increasingly anxious, he wrote to his friend Weliezko in 1897 :

« *Chaos reigns,*
Sleep is no longer the same : Something is
happening,
Someone is coming... »

<< *You may guess that by this "Someone", I mean **Antichrist himself**.* The end of the world is coming and I feel it blowing in my face, clear but elusive, just as the traveler, as he nears the sea, senses the sea air before he actually sees the surging waves. >>

To the same friend, he would make the following confidence in 1900, two months before his death : << The current state of the Church leads me to expect a terrible disappointment. I would be surprised even to see the liturgy remaining safe and triumphant. I sense the coming of a time when Christians will have to meet for prayer in the catacombs [what a prophecy, seventeen years before the Bolshevik Revolution !]. Everywhere the faith will be persecuted, perhaps less brutally than in the days of Nero, but more subtly and cruelly : *through lies, deception and misrepresentation*. And that is hardly an overstatement. Can you not see what is afoot? I see it clearly and have done so for a long while now! >>

Under an amiable exterior and pleasant words Soloviev tried to hide the deep suffering consuming him and the dread gripping his heart like a vice. He wished to carry on fighting until the end.

HOW IS ONE TO RESIST THE ANTICHRIST?

In 1896, he wrote to his French friend Eugene Tavernier a letter containing a programme which the Abbé de Nantes summarises in three points :

1. To develop the perfect Christian doctrine so that, in the times of the Apocalypse, the Gospel might be preached with such luminous clarity that each nation, each person, will be able to choose his camp in perfect knowledge of the facts, and preferably the camp of Christ the King! Soloviev would employ himself feverishly in this ultimate elucidation of the divine Wisdom, and from this would result the wonderful aesthetics and " Theurgy " found in *The Justification of the Good* (1897). To justify the good, the true and the beautiful is to put to work the divine energies of the Holy Spirit, who overcomes egoism and autolatry through charity and the self–renunciation of the saints.

2. During the predicted persecutions and apostasy, to cease << pursuing the power and grandeur of theocracy as the direct and immediate end of Christian politics >>. However, << *to consolidate the moral and religious unity of true believers, united around Rome, the definitive criterion being an attachment to the truth* >>, a truth that sets the elect apart from renegades and excites in them a horror of the false union formed by the latter around the Antichrist.

3. Lastly, *to combat the Adversary with the arms of light*, confident of the final triumph of those Christians who remain faithful, after a short but ferocious struggle which for a while will lead to an apparently universal victory by Hell. In this apocalyptic combat, the real victors will be the martyrs, and those who have << persevered until the

end >>.

THREE CONVERSATIONS

In 1899 Soloviev decided to describe the circumstances of this combat of the end times in *Three Conversations*. For him these constitute a kind of philosophical and spiritual last testament, as well as a *retractatio* where he wanted to return to the most cherished themes of his teachings in order to restate them and, if need be, correct them. Because of its eschatological character, this text is of capital importance. As our Abbé writes, << There is absolutely no way one can support and believe in Soloviev's *Theandry*, work actively on behalf of his *Theocracy* and share closely in his *Theurgy*, without clearly distinguishing these from what is currently their most dangerous caricature : the Antichrist at war against the Church. >>

Perhaps even within her very bosom...

With the rigor and intellectual agility so characteristic of him, Soloviev broaches the most fundamental questions for faith and morals : the end of history, the choice between Christ and Antichrist, and the problem of Evil. The literary genre adopted – that of *philosophical conversations* modeled on Plato's *Dialogues*, of which the philosopher had recently published a new translation – is more accessible and attractive than the theoretical treaty. It allows the author to be understood by a wider number of people.

He himself explains in his preface, dated << Easter Sunday 1900 >>, the aim of these conversations : << *I wanted, in so far as I could, to set out clearly how the problem of evil is addressed by vital aspects of Christian truth, aspects on which a thick fog is descending from various sides, especially in these latter times.* >> The parable accompanying his statement is quite delightful, and its lesson unexpected to say the least. Judge for yourself :

« PREACHERS OF EMPTINESS »

<< Many years ago, I happened to read about a new religion that had arisen somewhere in the eastern provinces. This religion, whose followers are called " hole–drillers " or " hole–worshippers ", consisted in drilling a medium-sized hole in some dark corner of their isba and then putting their mouths to it and repeating indefinitely : " My isba, my hole, save me! " Never before, it seems, had the object of worship attained such a degree of simplicity. But if the deification of a poor

peasant isba and of the simple opening made by human hands in its wall was a manifest aberration, it must however be said that it was an honest error : these men may have been absolutely mad but they did not deceive anybody, for they called their isba an *isba*, and the place they had drilled in the wall they rightly called a *hole*.

<< But the religion of the hole–worshippers rapidly experienced an " evolution " and underwent a "transformation". Despite its new look, this religion still retained its defective religious conceptions and scant philosophical interests, it kept its crass realism, but it had lost its previous honesty : their isba had now been given the title of "Kingdom of God on earth", and the hole had started to be called a "new Gospel", but the difference between this so–called gospel and the true one was exactly the same as that between a hole drilled in a beam and a complete living tree...

<< Certain hole–worshippers – admittedly the "intelligent" ones – no longer called themselves "hole–worshippers" but Christians, and they called their preaching the Gospel, but in fact ***it was a Christianity without Christ, and a Gospel, i.e. Good News, without the only good worth proclaiming : without the real resurrection to the fullness of the blessed life***. In short, it was nothing but emptiness, just like the hole drilled in the peasant isba. >>

What made Soloviev especially indignant is that these so–called apostles cover this emptiness, the "hole" of their notions, with a << counterfeit Christian flag >> which seduces and misleads the "little ones", the humble, who still have a simple belief in Christ's Gospel :

<< In an age when certain people think and say under their breath that Christ is *obsolete*, that He is *passé*, or even that He never existed at all, that He is a myth imagined by the Apostle Paul, and when such people obstinately continue to pass themselves off as genuine Christians and cloak the preaching of their emptiness under words wrested from their true meaning, then indifference and haughty disdain are no longer an appropriate reaction. Now that the moral atmosphere has been infected with a systematic lie, the public conscience cries out for such evil deeds to be called by their true name. The true task of polemics in this case is not to refute a pseudo–religion but to expose a veritable deception. >>

These " preachers of emptiness " claim Christ as their authority, but the true Christ is entirely alien to them, He is of no use to them and even constitutes an obstacle for them. Let them come clean and claim another

Master, Buddha for instance !

<< If human weakness makes these people experience an irresistible need to base their conviction not only on their own " reasoning " but also on some historical authority, why, I ask, do they not look in history for someone else who would be a more suitable representative? And in fact there is such a person, ready made for them, the founder of that widely popular religion which is **Buddhism**. Buddha really did preach what they are looking for : non–resistance to evil, impassivity and inactivity, sobriety, etc. And he succeeded, even without martyrdom, " in opening up a brilliant career " for his religion. The sacred books of the Buddhists really do proclaim *emptiness* and, to make these books fully agree with the new preaching on this matter, one would only need to simplify a few details. ***On the other hand, the Holy Scriptures of the Jews and the Christians are filled, are indeed wholly permeated, by a positive spiritual message that denies emptiness, both ancient and modern.*** To associate the preaching of emptiness with some statement found in the Gospel or the Prophets, they use all kinds of tricks to try and divorce this statement from its immediate context and indeed from the rest of the book. >>

Without actually naming his adversary, because of the censure that would have prevented the latter from replying, Soloviev, with a very sure instinct, crossed swords with Tolstoy, the prophet of non–violence and of nonresistance to evil, a veritable << lie of Antichrist >> and the most powerful, perhaps, of his precursors.

TOLSTOY'S FALSE GOSPEL

THE RUSSIAN LUTHER

Who today remembers the author of *War and Peace, Anna Karenina* and *Resurrection*? For his contemporary Soloviev, Lev Nicolayevich Tolstoy was a perverter of the Russian soul, more dangerous even than Marx and Nietzsche, because he propagated << a Christianity without dogma and a morality without strength, a morality that was purely sentimental, ostensibly virtuous but in reality quietist and, on that account, vicious >> (English CRC no 153, p. 37). He reduced everything to the single law of love, in the name of which he indiscriminately condemned his country's institutions, war in all its forms, the sciences and the arts.

<< Tolstoy is the Russian exemplar of the corruption of Christian thought >>, writes Father Rouleau in the introduction to the *Three Conversations*, << the falsifier of the whole Russian Orthodox tradition : **he represents the typical Russian heretic**, one who brings together every facet of both national greatness and weakness with an incomparable intensity and richness. In a way, Tolstoy is another Luther or a Russian Calvin! >>

Dostoevsky had already experienced a kind of revulsion for this "heretic" : << Their ideas, their manner of seeing things were completely opposed >>, recounts the Russian novelist's daughter... << A true patriot, a respectful son of the Church, a Slav faithful to the cause of the people of his race, Dostoevsky lived as a European, regarded Europe as his second home and never ceased advising those who came to ask his opinion to study, to read and to acquire that European culture which was so lacking among the majority of my compatriots.

<< Tolstoy's outlook was totally different. He loved Russia as sincerely as Dostoevsky did, but he would not judge her. On the other hand, he scorned European culture and regarded the ignorance of the mujiks as the supreme wisdom. He admired their defects, shared their childish nonsense, their ingenuous dream of a primitive communism. This apostle of defeatism advised his disciples to lay their weapons down before the enemy, not to fight against evil, to let it invade the world, and to leave the job of fighting this evil in the hands of God. ***He worked for the triumph of the Bolsheviks and naively claimed to be preaching Christian ideas***. >> (*Life of Dostoevsky by his daughter*, Paris, 1926, p. 289)

Aimee Dostoevsky attributes this disparity to Count Tolstoy's Germanic origins : << Tolstoy's German roots might explain the otherwise inexplicable and bizarre aspects of his character, his Protestant reflections on the Christ of Orthodoxy, his liking for a simple life of labour, very rare for Russians of his class, his extraordinary insensitivity to the sufferings of the Slavs tortured by the Turks, something which absolutely astonished my father. "How can he not feel pity? It is a mystery to me", he wrote in his *Diary of a Writer*. Tolstoy rejected science, culture and European literature in their entirety. "My faith", "my confession", he wrote at the top of his religious ramblings, in his evident desire to create a Kultur of *Jasnaya Poliana.* >> (p. 299)

Soloviev went much further than his master Dostoevsky in denouncing the prophet of non–violence as a precursor of the Antichrist. << With a genius of which I know no equal >>, writes our Abbé, << he turns our attention away from the noisy forerunners of the Bolsheviks, Marx and

Nietzsche, those inflammatory demons whom we know only too well, in order to focus our attention on a much less noisy figure, one who inspires no fear at all, on the contrary! but who is all the more dangerous for the charm with which he seduces souls, using flattering illusions that resemble the most stirring truths of Christianity. It is like two angels who resemble one another *"to the point of deceiving, if that were possible, the elect themselves"*, an angel of darkness on one side against an angel of light on the other : **Leo Tolstoy in all his glory! against Soloviev the "strastoterpstsi", the innocent persecuted for the love of Christ.** >> (English CRC n° 153, p. 37)

But let us take up the *Three Conversations* at the point where Soloviev has Tolstoy appear under the guise of an ostensibly evangelical "Prince" who is successively confronted by three characters : a general, a diplomat and a mysterious Mr Z, who is none other than Soloviev himself. The conversation turns on the general theme : *Should one resist evil?*

A "GLORIOUS AND CHRIST–LOVING ARMY"

In the first conversation, the general replies *yes* to this question, in accordance with the principle that civilized countries have always opposed evil **with armed force**. This officer represents << the moral religious point of view, which belongs to the past >>, Soloviev explains in his preface. His nephew, Sergius Soloviev, recounts that, when his uncle read his manuscript to his close friends and family for the first time, << the general's remarks were pronounced with an ardor that betrayed his love for the old soldier. His own grandfather and godfather had been an admiral, and he counted many friends in the army. >> (p. 435)

Our general complains that the title "glorious and Christ–loving Army" traditionally given to the Russian Army and the military profession in general are presently disdained by politicians and vilified by base pacifist campaigns. Confronting the Tolstoyan prince who upholds the new Gospel that *Evil must be vanquished by good, God is not found in force but in justice, you shall not kill*, etc., the general protests that justice must be backed up by force if it is to be exercised in an efficacious manner, be it only to defend innocent victims!

In support of his claims, he recounts that one day he had exterminated in an instant no less than a thousand bashibazouks (Turkish mercenaries) who had been indulging in abominable cruelties against the unhappy Armenians. Not only did he feel no remorse over this, but he remembered it as << a luminous Easter of the soul >>, with the satisfaction of a duty accomplished for << *the faith, the tsar and the fatherland* >>. The Prince then reproaches him for not having conducted himself, in the circumstances, in a rather more "evangelical" manner :

<< THE PRINCE. – He who is truly filled with an authentic evangelical spirit will find within himself, when the need arises, the facility of using words, gestures and his aspect to influence his poor ignorant brother who wishes to commit a crime or some other guilty act. He is able to create such a startling impression on him that he immediately recognizes his fault and forsakes the path of error.

THE GENERAL. – Saints in heaven! Are you really advising me that before the bashibazouks who were roasting little children, I should have made some touching gestures and pronounced a few touching words?

MR Z. – Words, perhaps, would not have been quite appropriate owing to the intervening distance and the fact that neither of you understood the other's language. And as for gestures calculated to make a startling impression, you may think what you like, but nothing could have been more fitting in the precise circumstances than rounds of shells fired.

LADY. – Really, what language and what instruments could the general have used to make himself understood by the bashibazouks?

THE PRINCE. – I never said that *they* could have acted in an evangelical manner towards the bashibazouks. What I said was that a person full of the authentic Gospel spirit would have found a way, in this case as in any other, to awaken in these blind souls the good which lies hidden in every human creature.

MR Z. – Do you really think so?

THE PRINCE. – I have not the slightest doubt about it.

MR Z. – Well, do you think then that Christ was sufficiently imbued with the authentic Gospel spirit?

THE PRINCE. – What is the significance of this question?

MR Z. – It signifies that I wish to know why Christ did not use the power of the Gospel spirit to awaken the good hidden in the souls of Judas, Herod, the Jewish high priests and lastly of the impenitent thief whom people completely forget when they speak about his good comrade. For the positive Christian conception, there is no insurmountable difficulty in this [...]. You may twist and disfigure all you like the text of the Four Gospels, but the facts will remain no less undeniable, and this is the very essence of our argument, that **Christ suffered cruel persecutions and was put to death precisely because His enemies hated Him**. The fact that He

Himself remained morally superior to all this, that He chose not to resist and forgave His enemies, is easy to understand, both from both my point of view and yours. But, why, in pardoning His enemies, did He not – to adopt your language – free their souls from the appalling darkness in which they were stagnating? Why did He not vanquish their wickedness with the power of His gentleness? Why did He not awaken the good that lay dormant in them, why did He not enlighten and regenerate their minds? In a word, why did He not act on Judas, Herod and the Jewish high priests as He acted on the good thief and on him alone? Once again : either He was unable to do so or He did not wish to. In either case it is evident, according to your argument, that He was insufficiently imbued with the true Gospel spirit; and since we are talking, if I am not mistaken, about the Gospel of Christ and of no one else, it would appear that for you Christ was insufficiently imbued with the authentic spirit of Christ. Congratulations! >>

The prince is unable to reply; he is beaten on the basis of his own principles...

THE CULTURE OF PEACE AND PROGRESS

The second conversation calls on the politician, the professional diplomat. His speeches were read by Soloviev, according to his nephew, << in the artificial voice of an elderly smug bureaucrat, mimicking the minister Goremkim >> (p. 435). This representative << of the progress of the dominant culture of the day >> claims to overcome evil not by force as in barbarian times, but *by instruction, by the revelation to backward peoples of ideology and modern techniques*. He is persuaded that material and cultural progress will dispel misery and ignorance, the cause of all ills...

The prince, who is present at this conversation, says not a word, presumably finding some support for his own views in it. Our fine speaker then uses the example of the Germany of William II, who sought to shake Turkey out of its lethargy by eliminating illiteracy and constructing the Berlin–Baghdad railway. All this was done without anyone worrying about religion or having any misgivings that imperialism might be the real underlying reason for such development aid. One might think one was listening to one of our contemporary politicians : << Authentic culture demands the complete disappearance of all conflict between men and nations. The politics of peace is the criterion and symptom of the progress of civilization, etc. >> Mgr Rupp cannot restrain his applause : << It is a kind of prelude to the great pontifical document *Populorum progressio.* >>

As for Soloviev, he seldom intervenes in this conversation, except at the end where he reduces the beautiful construction of his interlocutor to smoke :

<< Mr Z. – Regarding your remarks about the politics of peace being a symptom of progress, I recall that in Turgenev's "Smoke", one of the characters says with great justice : "Progress is a symptom!" Does it not follow then that the politics of peace is a symptom of a symptom?

THE POLITICIAN. – Yes. But what does that prove? Clearly, everything is relative. But what exactly is your point?

Mr Z. – Well, if the politics of peace is only the shadow of a shadow, is there any reason to talk about it so much? All this talk about the progress of a shadow? Would it not be much better to say openly to humanity what Father Barsanophius said to the pious lady : "You are old, you are weak, and you will never get better." >>

In fact, the politician's speech, replacing God and the Good with culture and peace, is too *secularist* for Soloviev not to find it unbearable. Conclusion : armed force against evil is necessary, yes, in the immediate term! Instruction and development are also highly praiseworthy, in the medium term. But against moral evil, against Tolstoy who disarms consciences, against the Antichrist << behind whom lurks an abyss of evil >>, neither remedy is sufficient.

THE COMBAT OF THE END TIMES

A third and final talk is now provided in magisterial fashion by Mr Z., Soloviev's mouthpiece, << promoter of that absolute religion which is to reveal its decisive importance in the future >>, as indicated in the preface... For *absolute religion* we should read *integral religion*, because it integrates every sphere of human activity, and puts each thing, each event in its place, through the judgment that will take place at the end of time. This positive supernatural vision of universal history justifies and reconciles the occasionally contradictory views of the politician and the general : << The warrior's sword and the diplomat's pen should both be esteemed insofar as they actually correspond to the objective in such or such a situation, and the most fitting instrument on each occasion is the one whose use is most appropriate, that is to say which serves the good with the greatest success. >>

Now, the true religion reveals that at the end of time the Antichrist will appear, the ultimate manifestation of evil in history, and that after a brief triumph, he will experience his final downfall. Soloviev now goes right to the heart of the matter :

<< MR Z. – There can be no doubt that this reign of the Antichrist, which according to the Bible – both Old and New Testaments – will mark the final act of the historical tragedy, will not simply be one of unbelief or materialism or the negation of Christianity, etc., but will be *a religious imposture*, and that the name of Christ will then be usurped by forces within humanity which, in reality and in their very essence, are alien and positively inimical to Christ and His Spirit. >>

Some of the Fathers of the Church had foreseen this before Soloviev: << Saint John Damascene insists on the hypocrisy of the Antichrist: " As a prelude to his reign, or rather to his tyranny, *he will feign holiness...*" These are the characteristics one finds in the writings of Saint Hippolytus who calls him " the deceiver ", and in Saint Cyril of Jerusalem for whom the Antichrist " will feign prudence, pious clemency and philanthropy ". >> (B. Marchadier, *Ecumenism and Eschatology according to Soloviev*, Paris, 1994, p. 158) Because the Antichrist will disguise himself under the very features of Christ and caricature His universal work of reconciliation, the whole power of the authentic Word of God, sharp as a sword, will be needed to expose him :

<<MR Z. – Of all the stars that rise on the mental horizon of one who makes a close study of our Sacred Books, there is not, I think, any more luminous or striking than that which shines out in these words of the Gospel : " *Do you think that I have come to bring peace to the world? No, I tell you, but division*. " He came to bring Truth on earth and, like the good, it is before all else a force of division.

LADY. – That needs explaining. For why in that case is Christ called the *Prince of peace*, and why did He say that peacemakers would be called *sons of God?*

MR Z. – Am I to understand that you wish me to take on the supreme dignity of reconciling these contradictory texts?

LADY. – Precisely so !

MR Z. – Observe then that the only way they can be reconciled is by separating good peace, or true peace, from bad peace, or false peace. And this separation is directly pointed out to us by Him who brought us both true peace and honest enmity : " *I leave you peace. My own peace I give you. I do not give it as the world gives it*. " There is therefore a good peace of Christ, a peace founded on the division which Christ came to bring on earth, namely the division between good and evil, lies and Truth;

and there is a bad peace, a peace of the world, founded on confusion or the external union of what is, internally, at war.

LADY. – So how do you propose to show us the difference between the good and the bad peace?

MR Z. – A little like the general did the day before yesterday when he jocularly remarked that there are good peaces, like that of Nystad or Kuchuk Kainarji [two peace treaties granting Russia extensive access rights to the Baltic and the Black Sea in the eighteenth century]. Behind the jocularity there lies a more general and important meaning. In spiritual warfare, as in politics, a good peace is that which is only concluded when the object of the war is accomplished. >>

THE RESURRECTION, A STUMBLING BLOCK

What is the point in searching for " the pure moral good ", as the tolstoyan Prince seeks to do, or working indefinitely for the progress of humanity, as the politician demands, if the final result is the death of every man, barbarian and civilized alike! And if, again, Christ and His disciples, having fully accomplished "the demands of the good", suffered death and did not actually rise again, – as Tolstoy claimed in a book antiphrastically entitled "Resurrection", which was published in the same year as *Three Conversations!* – then the Kingdom of God is nothing but a kingdom of death.

Against this nonsense, inspired by an all–pervasive modernism, Soloviev opposes his luminous faith in the Resurrection of Christ, the sign and promise of the final resurrection of the elect, and of their victory over the Antichrist :

<<MR Z. – We have but one defense against despair: ***actual resurrection***. We know that the fight between good and evil not only takes place in souls and society but even, at a deeper level, in the physical world. And we already know that in the past the good principle won a victory over life, in a personal resurrection. We await one thing only : further victories involving the collective resurrection of all. And here even evil finds its meaning, the final explanation of its being, in that it serves to realize and enhance the ever greater triumph of good. If death is more powerful than mortal life, resurrection to eternal life is even more powerful than either of them. The Kingdom of God is the reign of life which has triumphed through the resurrection, and it is in this life that there lies the real, actual and final good. Here lies all the power, all the work of Christ, here is manifest His true love for us, and our love for Him. All the rest is but a condition, a means, a path. Without faith in the resurrection

accomplished by One alone and without hope in the future resurrection of all, any talk of some unspecified Kingdom of God is nothing but words and only leads to the kingdom of death. >>

Around this fundamental truth of our faith, our Abbé magisterially contrasts the two protagonists of the drama : << *One* [Soloviev] *believed that Jesus Christ, the true Son of God made man, risen from the dead, had had a substantial effect on the world and divinized it through the Church, the Roman Church!* He exhorted the Russian people to **entrust themselves unreservedly to the grace of Jesus**, to accept the self-renunciation, sacrifice and humility demanded by the Gospel, and to return to visible Catholic Unity! He encouraged them to struggle with all their might against Evil, particularly against any kind of schism or revolution... *The other* [Tolstoy] *denied the resurrection of Jesus and His divinity*; he made man responsible for perfecting and divinising himself by following the impulses of his heart, **by not resisting evil**, on the contrary by yielding to it. In this way he aspired to lead mankind without encumbrance to happiness, peace, fraternity and the equal wellbeing of all... >> (English CRC n° 153, p. 37)

THE SACRED IMAGE OF CHRIST

Soloviev wrote in his *Foundations of the Spiritual Life* (1884) : << I would advise everyone to undertake this type of examination of conscience which does not deceive : **to take the image of Christ as the measure of our conscience**. In moments of doubt, when there at least remains the possibility of reasoning with oneself and of meditating, remember Christ, place Him before you as though He were truly Alive, as indeed He is, and lay on Him the whole weight of your doubt. He is already predisposed to take on Himself the burdens of others, not of course to free your hands so that you may commit some iniquitous act, but in order that, by turning to Him and relying on Him, you may abstain from evil and that, in this difficult case, you may become the instrument of His indubitable Justice. >> (quoted by Mgr Rupp, p. 179)

THE CONDEMNATIONS OF SAINT PIUS X

We wish to draw your attention, Venerable Brethren, to *this distortion of the Gospel and of the sacred character of Our Lord Jesus Christ*, God and Man, which is practiced within the "Sillon" and elsewhere. As soon as the social question is raised, it is the fashion in certain quarters first to put aside the divinity of Jesus Christ and then only to talk of His infinite mercy, His compassion for all human misery, and His pressing exhortations to love of neighbor and fraternity. True, Jesus loved us with an immense, infinite love, and He came on earth to suffer and die so that, gathered around Him in justice and love, and motivated by the same sentiments of mutual charity, all men might live in peace and felicity.

But for the realization of this temporal and eternal happiness, He has laid down with supreme authority *the condition that we must belong to His flock, that we must accept His doctrine, that we must practice virtue, and that we must accept the teaching and guidance of Peter and his successors*. Further, whilst Jesus was kind to sinners and to those who went astray, He did not respect their false ideas, however sincere they might have appeared. He loved them all, but He instructed them in order to convert them and save them. If He called to Himself, that He might comfort them, those who toiled and suffered, it was not to preach to them the jealousy of a chimerical equality. If He lifted up the lowly, it was not to instil in them the sentiment of a dignity independent from and rebellious to the duty of obedience. If His heart overflowed with gentleness for souls of good will, He could also arm Himself with holy indignation against those who profaned the House of God, against the wretched men who scandalize the little ones, against the authorities who crush the people with the weight of heavy burdens without ever lifting a finger to ease them. He was as strong as He was gentle. He reproved, threatened and chastised, knowing and teaching us that fear is the beginning of wisdom, and that it is sometimes fitting for a man to cut off an offending limb to save his body. Finally, He did not announce for future society the reign of an ideal happiness from which suffering would be banished; but, through His teachings and through His example, He traced the path of the happiness that is possible on earth and of the perfect happiness in Heaven : **the royal way of the Cross**. *These are teachings that one would be wrong to apply solely to one's personal life in order to merit eternal salvation; these are eminently social teachings, and they show in Our Lord Jesus Christ something quite different from a humanitarianism that lacks both substance and authority.*

SAINT PIUS X, *Letter on the Sillon*, 25 August 1910, n° 42.

It was armed with the *labarum* of the Holy Face of Jesus that our prophet drew the portrait of the Antichrist in the concluding part of his *Three Conversations* : << ***To reveal in advance the face of deception behind which hides an abyss of evil, such was my overriding intention in writing this little book.*** >> We must now meditate on this " Short Story of the Antichrist ", the account of the Russian monk *Pansophius*, whose Greek name means *all wisdom*, and who undoubtedly represents Soloviev himself.

THE RISE AND FALL OF THE ANTICHRIST

IN THOSE TIMES...

The account starts by recalling the events that are to precede the coming of the Antichrist : << *The 20th century after the birth of Christ will be a time of the greatest wars, of civil strife and revolutions.* >> For something written in 1900, it is not a bad prognosis! The first part of the century will see the West invaded by the yellow peoples under the banner of Pan–Mongolism, then their retreat and the creation of the United States of Europe (!) instigated by freemasonry. The Jews will return to Palestine and repopulate it... Material prosperity will then spread throughout all civilized countries. << The final decline of theoretical materialism >> will free minds from this mental straitjacket but, in its place, the majority will be satisfied with a confused system of beliefs, lacking any clearly defined dogma or practice.

<< At that time [we are now at the beginning of the 21st century], there was among the few believing spiritualists a remarkable man – many called him a superman – who was as far removed from the childhood of understanding as he was from that of the heart. He was still a young man, but his superior genius had earned him at the age of thirty a widespread reputation as a great thinker, writer and public figure. Conscious of possessing within himself a powerful spiritual force, he had shown himself to be a convinced spiritualist, and his keen intellect had always shown him the truth of those things that should be believed in : the Good, God and the Messiah. ***In these he believed, but he loved only himself. He believed in God but in the depths of his heart he could not prevent himself from preferring himself.*** He believed in the Good, but the omniscient eye of the Eternal knew that this man would bow down before the power of Evil as soon as he felt its allure... >>

This "son of God", on whom so many gifts had been lavished, will however lack those of humility and gratitude. Nor will wisdom be his, since he will not even practice its beginning, which is the fear of God (Prov 1:7). The psychological portrait that Soloviev draws here is gripping, particularly as it conforms so closely to what Scripture and the most ancient Tradition say on the matter. Note that this extraordinary man will not have a proper name or a country : he will be *a disincarnate being*, the opposite of Christ who Himself became incarnate. His pride will lead him to view himself as the equal of Christ, << His forerunner >>, and then to place himself above Him and finally supplant Him, as a new Mohammed – the comparison is Soloviev's :

<< This man will place himself above Christ, justifying this by the following chain of reasoning : "Christ, by preaching and accomplishing in his life the moral good, was the *reformer* of humanity, but my role is to be the *benefactor* of this same humanity, partly reformed and partly incapable of being reformed. I will give men everything they need. Christ, as a moralist, divided men in terms of good and evil, whereas I will unite them with benefits which are necessary to good and evil alike. I will be the true representative of this God who makes his sun to rise on both the righteous and the sinner. **Christ brought the sword, I will bring peace**. He threatened earth with the last judgment, but I will be the last judge, and my judgment will not only be one of justice but also of charity. There will also be justice in my judgment, but it will not be a retributive justice but a distributive one. I will make a distinction between each man and I will give each what is appropriate to him." >>

THE HOUR OF SATAN

Privately persuaded that the hour of God is about to sound for him, – he is the same age as Christ –, << this just man full of pride awaits the sanction from the Most High before undertaking the salvation of humanity... but he can see no sign of it. He is already thirty, and a further three years pass by. And then a thought crosses his mind, penetrating him like a shiver to the marrow of his bones: "And what if...? What if it were not me, but the other... the Galilean? What if He were not my forerunner, but the true one, the first and the last? In that case He must still be alive... But where is He then? And what if He were to come to me... here, at this very moment... What would I say to him? would I have to bow before Him like the least Christian imbecile and mumble stupidly like a Russian peasant : *Lord Jesus Christ, have pity on me a sinner*, or to stretch out my arms in the form of a cross like some Polish woman? No, I am a luminous genius, a superman, never!"

<< Then, instead of the cold reasoned respect he formerly had for God and Christ, there arose and grew in his heart at first a kind of terror, and then a burning envy which compressed and contracted his whole being, and finally a deadly hatred which made him quite breathless : *"it is me, me, **ME**, not him!* He does not count among the living, and will never count among them. He is not risen, no, no, no! He rotted, He rotted in the tomb, He rotted like the last..." And frothing at the mouth, he rushed convulsively out of his home, jumped over the garden wall and fled, along a rocky path, into the black night...

<< His fury abated and gave way to despair that was as cold and heavy as those rocks and as sombre as that night. He stopped at the edge of a precipitous ravine, from the bottom of which he could hear the muffled sound of a torrent running over the stones. An overpowering anguish pressed upon his heart. Suddenly, something stirred within him. " Should I call him and ask him what I must do? " And in the darkness an image, gentle and sad, appeared to him. " *He has pity on me... Oh, no, never! He did not rise, no, no!* " And he hurled himself into the ravine. But something supple, like a column of water, held him up in the air. He felt a sort of electrical discharge, and a force threw him backwards. He lost consciousness for a moment and then found himself kneeling a few paces away from the ravine. Before him could be made out a silhouette which gave off a murky phosphorescent light. Two eyes could be made out, and their unbearable glare pierced his heart... >> Satan, for it was him, then comes up to the one he calls his " only son " and, having adorned him with beauty, fills him with his power.

THE CONQUEST OF THE WORLD

From that day, he will go on to conquer the world at a rapid rate. Nothing will stand in the way of this easy–going, happy, smiling man. He will write a book entitled *"The Open Path to Universal Peace and Prosperity"*, which will earn him the approval of all.

<< This path had a universal character and ***abolished all contradictions***. It united a noble respect for ancient traditions and symbols with a broad and daring radicalism in socio–political questions. Its boundless freedom of thought was allied with the most profound appreciation for everything mystical; its unmistakable individualism was united with an ardent zeal for the common good; and the guiding principles of the most sublime idealism went hand in hand with extremely precise, practical solutions for daily life. And all this was blended and cemented

with such artistic genius that every thinker and every man of action, no matter how narrow–minded he might have been, had no difficulty in viewing and accepting the whole from his own personal standpoint, for ***there was no requirement for him to make any sacrifice to truth itself, to actually rise above his own ego***, to renounce in any way his narrow–mindedness, to correct anything false in his views and aspirations or to supplement their deficiencies. >>

Herein lies the mark of the Antichrist denounced by Soloviev. This Man will claim to reconcile opposites and to satisfy the desires of each and every person without anyone having to agree to the least sacrifice. No need for "conversion", self–renunciation or the "narrow road", as the road will lay wide "open"! << Not only does this inspired author proclaim a universal "I understand you", but he surpasses everyone in his attachment to the values he defends. Polymorphic and omni–comprehensive, he is a traditionalist to traditionalists, a modernist to modernists, and a rationalist to rationalists. >> (Bernard Marchadier, *Soloviev's Ecumenism and Eschatology*, p. 162)

He will thus be celebrated as "the Great", "the Incomparable", "the Unique", because he will appear to succeed where all his predecessors had failed. All? Yes, even Christ... Moreover, the name of Jesus Christ does not even appear in this work, nor does that of the Virgin Mary, a distinctive sign of the Antichrist, but Soloviev foresees, alas! that very few Christians will take offence at this :

<< No doubt certain pious people, although heaping praise on the book, will nevertheless end up asking why Christ is not mentioned even once in it. But other Christians will retort : "Thank God! In past centuries, sacred things have already been sufficiently debased by every type of inopportune zealot, and nowadays a deeply religious writer must be extremely guarded in these matters. Given that the substance of the book is imbued with a true Christian spirit of active love and universal goodwill, what more could you want?" On this point everyone will agree. >>

A FALLACIOUS HARMONY

The brotherhood of the freemasons will recognize this astounding writer as one of their own and will elect him President for life of the United States of Europe, and then of the "World Standing Committee". Having become Lord of the world, another distinctive sign of the Antichrist! in the space of three years, he is now ready to put his new Gospel into practice.

In the course of a world Congress, he will begin by granting all peoples the peace to which they aspire : << International law at last has a sanction which it has hitherto lacked. From now on, no power will dare to say "war" when I say "peace". Peoples of the earth, peace be with you! >> The following year, having concentrated in his hands the entire system of world finances, he will offer them prosperity as well. Hence this new blasphemy : << Come to me now, all you who are hungry and cold, that I may feed and warm you. >> Finally, when the crowd start to demand magic tricks, he has a Magician come from the Far East and multiply miracles and wonders. << And the whole earth marveled and followed the Beast. >> (Ap. 13:3)

When the peace and freedom of all has been guaranteed, and respect shown to all cultures and religions, the superman will appear as the benefactor of humanity, the incomparable " defender of human rights " (Marchadier, p. 163). Yet he still does not accept Christ, He who said, << Without me, you can do nothing. >> This antinomy permits Soloviev to speak about a *"bogus good"*. And one does not have to wait long to see its fruits : << Under his reign, men will learn to love themselves, to admire and idolize themselves, not as the servants and living icons of Christ, but by usurping the place of God and forgetting the Lord. >> (English CRC n₀ 153, p. 39)

ECUMENICAL IMPOSTURE

The question of religion will still remain to be settled. The number of true believers will have diminished considerably, but their faith, strengthened by their struggles against an all–pervasive paganism, will be perceived by the Antichrist as an obstacle to his universal domination. He will then decide to convene an ecumenical council... in Jerusalem! The opening, fixed for 14 September, feast of the exaltation of the Holy Cross! will be very grand. One would think one was present at an assembly of the United Nations, or the World Council of Churches, or the meeting at... Assisi :

<< Two thirds of the immense temple devoted to the "unification of all cults" were laid out with benches and other seating arrangements for members of the congress. The remaining third was taken up by a high platform on which were placed the Emperor's throne and another throne a little lower down for the great magician [...]. ***The members of the congress had already celebrated their services in different churches***, and the opening of the congress was to have a character that was entirely secular. When the Emperor, accompanied by the great magician and his suite, made his entrance, the orchestra began to play "the March of United Humanity",

which was the international hymn of the Empire, and all the members rose to their feet, and, waving their hats, gave three enthusiastic cheers : "Vivat! Hurrah! Hoch!" The Emperor, standing by the throne and stretching out his hands with an air of majestic benevolence, proclaimed in a sonorous and pleasing voice :

<< Christians of all denominations! Brothers and beloved subjects! From the beginning of my reign, which the Most High has blessed with such wonderful and glorious deeds, I have had no cause to be dissatisfied with you; you have always fulfilled your duties true to your faith and your conscience. But this is still too little for me. My sincere love for you, beloved brothers, thirsts to be reciprocated. I want you to recognize in me your true leader in every enterprise undertaken for the good of humanity, and that not merely out of a sense of duty, but also out of a feeling of love that springs from the heart... Christians! Tell me what is the most precious thing for you in Christianity, so that I may direct my efforts to that end. >>

In pursuit of his design of universal reconciliation and peaceful coexistence "under his leadership", he proposes to Catholics to restore their leader to his see in Rome with all his ancient prerogatives, to the Orthodox attached to the symbols of their sacred tradition to create at Constantinople a world museum of Christian archaeology, and to Protestants to found a world Institute for the free study of the Scriptures. The immense majority of Christians from the three denominations rally enthusiastically to the Emperor's proposals and go up to sit on the platform at his side. << Below there remain only three groups of members, who now move more closely together and press around Starets John, Pope Peter and Professor Pauli. >>

THE DEATH OF THE TWO WITNESSES

<< The Emperor then addressed them in a saddened tone : " What else can I do for you, you strange people? What do you expect from me? Tell me, then, you Christians deserted by the majority of your brothers and your leaders, you who stand condemned by popular feeling : what is it that you value most in Christianity? "

<< At this Starets John rose up like a white candle and quietly answered : "Sire! ***What we value most in Christianity is Christ Himself***, from whom everything proceeds, for we know that in Him the whole plenitude of the Godhead has its bodily dwelling. From yourself, Sire, we are also ready to accept any gift, provided only that we can recognize the sacred hand of Christ in your generosity. Our candid answer to your question, what can you do for us, is this : Confess here and now before us that Jesus Christ is the Son of God

who came in the flesh, who rose and who will come again. Confess His name, and we will lovingly receive you as the true precursor of His second glorious coming."

<< He finished his speech and fixed his eyes on the face of the Emperor. The latter was experiencing a deep feeling of unease. A hellish storm was raging within him, like the one he had experienced on that fateful night [...]. Suddenly, he heard the unearthly voice he had heard before : "Keep silent and fear nothing." He remained silent. But his whole face, dark and icy, contracted and his eyes flashed. Meanwhile, as Starets John was still making his speech, the great magician, wrapped in the ample tricoloured mantle which covered his cardinal's purple, could be seen performing all kinds of manipulations beneath it. His eyes were fixed and flashing, and his lips moved slightly. Through the open windows of the temple one could see an immense black cloud approaching. Very soon, complete darkness had set in. Starets John had not taken his frightened eyes off the silent face of the Emperor. Suddenly, in horror, he sprang back and, turning round, cried out in a choked voice : "***My little children, behold the Antichrist!***" At that moment, a deafening thunderclap exploded, a great ball of fire burst into the temple and enveloped the Starets. For a moment everyone was completely stunned, and when the deafened Christians came to their senses, Starets John was lying dead on the ground. >>

The Emperor boasted before the Assembly that his father in heaven had avenged him by making << fire from heaven >> fall on his foolish opponent. << Suddenly a word, clear and distinct, rang out in the temple : "***Contradicitur*** ". Pope Peter rose, trembling with anger, and brandished his crosier in the direction of the Emperor : "We have no Lord but Jesus Christ, the Son of the living God! As for you, you have just heard who you are... By the authority of Christ, I, the servant of the servants of God, cast you out forever, foul dog, from the city of God, and I deliver you up to your father Satan! Anathema! Anathema! Anathema!" The roar of thunder covered the last anathema and the last Pope collapsed lifeless on the ground. "So die all my enemies by the arm of my Father!" cried the Emperor. "*Pereant, pereant*", exclaimed the trembling princes of the Church. >> And they all left the Temple.

ON A DARK NIGHT...

Professor Pauli, along with the last of the remaining Protestant faithful, join the Catholics and the Orthodox who have rebelled against the Antichrist. They carry off the bodies of the two Witnesses, the << ark of the last covenant >>, to the deserted heights of Jericho, while in Jerusalem the Emperor and his supporters noisily celebrate their victory by signing an "Act of Union of the Churches", cleverly seeking to abolish all the old quarrels of the past and to open up a great new epoch of Christian history, under the aegis of the Antichrist! It is the supreme deception.

But the two Witnesses rise from the dead, and there then takes place a touching scene of true ecumenism, of the kind that Soloviev had always longed for. Here he gives us the key to his own failure : the Antichrist had to come first, the one who would have the audacity to caricature the sacred Union of the Churches. This union will be realized as Christ promised, but only after each had chosen between the true faith and the falsification of the faith.

<< Having come back to life, Starets John said : "You see, my little children, that we have not parted after all! This then is what I have to tell you : the time has come to realize the last prayer of Christ who prayed that His disciples should all be *one*, even as He Himself is *one* with the Father. To achieve this unity in Christ, my little children, let us honor our beloved brother Peter. From now on let him pasture Christ's flocks. Yes, brothers!" And he embraced Peter. Then Professor Pauli came up in his turn : "*Tu es Petrus*", he declared to the Pope. "This has now been thoroughly proved and placed beyond a shadow of a doubt." And he clasped Peter's hand firmly, while he held out his left hand to Starets John saying : "Now then, dear Father, we are *one* in Christ."

<< In this manner, the unification of Churches took place on a dark night in a high and deserted spot. But the nocturnal darkness was suddenly illuminated by a brilliant light, and **a great sign appeared in the heavens : a Woman, clothed in the sun with the moon beneath Her feet and a crown of twelve stars on Her head**. The apparition remained motionless for some time, and then began to move slowly towards the south. Pope Peter raised his crosier and exclaimed : "Behold our standard! Let us follow it!" And he departed in the direction of the apparition, accompanied by the two old men and the whole crowd of Christians, all making their way towards God's mountain, Sinai... >>

Thus ends the manuscript of Fr Pansophius, but Soloviev goes on. According to his holy friend, he says, although the Jews will have strongly contributed to the Antichrist's success, it will be they who give the final signal for an uprising against the false Messiah. It will then be seen << that Israel's soul, in its inmost depths, does not live by calculations and the avarice of Mammon, but by the power of a profound sentiment, that of its hope and vehement undying faith in the Messiah >>, and Soloviev prayed ardently for this until his dying day! The Antichrist will want to crush these last surviving opponents, but will be engulfed along with his whole army in an ocean of fire, and then Christ will be seen descending on His elect << in His royal vestments, with the wounds of the nails in His outstretched hands >>.

UNDER THE STANDARD OF THE IMMACULATE

Saint Paul had warned his Christians : << Before the Coming of Our Lord Jesus Christ and our gathering around Him... there must come the apostasy and be revealed *the man of lawlessness, the son of perdition*, who opposes and sets himself above everything that bears the name of God or sacred object, *even going so far as to take his seat in the sanctuary of God*, proclaiming himself to be God... And you also know what is presently holding him back, preventing him from appearing before his appointed time. >> (2 Th 2.1–7) Certain Fathers of the Church have seen in the mysterious obstacle holding the Antichrist back the infallible power of the Roman papacy. And the Orthodox Soloviev wrote : << As there is in this world but one legitimate and traditional centre of unity, namely Rome, it follows that in order to fight with Jesus Christ against the Antichrist, genuine believers must rally round this centre... >> But he added, << ... to the degree indicated by their consciences. I know that there are priests and monks who think otherwise and who demand that we should unreservedly abandon ourselves to ecclesiastical authority, as though to God. This is an error which will have to be termed a heresy when it is clearly formulated. **One must expect that 99% of all priests and monks will declare themselves for the Antichrist. That is their own affair...** >> (English CRC n° 115, p. 19)

For his part Mgr Rupp writes : << There are, within Christendom, certain viewpoints which are the hallmark of the Antichrist or antichrists. They are characterized by their lack of honesty and the cloak they cast over their true nature. They need to be exposed, under the sign of the gigantic battle raging between Christ and the preternatural Enemy. >> (*The Ecclesial Message of Soloviev*, p. 368) Now, Mgr Rupp's whole aim throughout the 600 pages of this book is to show that the new religion resulting from Vatican II has a strange resemblance to Soloviev's marvellous theosophy, and that the United Nations is an outline of its sacred Theocracy!

Our Abbé asked in 1978 : << Given this *strange resemblance* as well as the new religion's perfect identity with Soloviev's Antichrist, whose *resemblance* to Christ lends him all his charm and prestige, the question arises : *Are we living through the dream of the saintly Soloviev or that of the demoniacal Tolstoy? Are we in the times of Christ's victory or in the times of the Antichrist?* >> (English CRC n° 132, p. 14) And today, does the " dream " of unity cherished by John Paul II come from Christ or from His Adversary?

The Secret of Fatima must decide between us. The Virgin Mary did not come to reveal to us some wondrous plan of Peace, Justice and universal Progress for all peoples of the world. Instead She showed three little children hell << *where the souls of poor sinners go* >>; She requested that Russia be consecrated to Her Immaculate Heart in order that it might be << *converted* >>; and finally She announced that there would be a return to the time of the martyrs, put to death in the wake of a mysterious << *bishop dressed in white* >>.

In Soloviev's account, the two Witnesses of the Apocalypse who died and rose again are the representatives of the Churches of the East and West. How can we not think of Pope John Paul I and the Patriarch Nikodim who both died in September 1978. Likewise, Soloviev remarks that the appearance of the << Woman clothed in the sun >> took place three day after the Antichrist's disastrous council, that is to say on 17 September, the day when the Russian Church celebrates the holy martyr *Sophia*, the figure of the Immaculate! Let us conclude with our Abbé : << It is You O Queen who turn our eyes away from the seductions of the Serpent. Your secret, at last revealed, is that of a Creature forgetful of Herself and preserved for God Alone, a Creature whom God has magnificently exalted. *Your lesson saves us from the mirages of the Antichrist who is Your total antithesis.* >> (*Letter to my Friends* n° 179, 15 August 1964)

Brother Thomas of Our Lady of Perpetual Succor.

Vladimir Soloviev on God Using Unbelievers

Those who feel horrified at the thought that the Spirit of Christ acts through men who do not believe in Him, are wrong even from the dogmatic point of view.

When an unbelieving priest correctly celebrates the liturgy, Christ is present in the sacrament in spite of the celebrant's unbelief and unworthiness, for the sake of the people who need it.

If the Spirit of Christ can act through an unbelieving priest in a sacrament of the Church, why can it not act in history through unbelieving agents, especially when the believers drive it away? The Spirit bloweth where it listeth. Its enemies may well serve it.

Christ who has commanded us to love our enemies can certainly not only love them Himself but also know how to use them for His work. And nominal Christians who pride themselves on having the same kind of faith as the devils should call to mind another thing in the Gospel — the story of two apostles, Judas Iscariot and Thomas. Judas greeted Christ with words and with a kiss. Thomas declared his unbelief in Him to His face. But Judas betrayed Christ and 'went and hanged himself,' and Thomas remained an apostle and died for Christ.

—— Vladimir Solovyov, "The Collapse of the Mediaeval World-Conception," pp. 60 – 71 in *A Solovyov Anthology*. Trans. Natalie Duddington (New York: Charles Scribner's Sons, 1950), 70.

Vladimir Sergeyevich Soloviev on the Antichrist

By Giacomo Cardinal Biffi

Vladimir Sergeyevich Soloviev passed away 100 years ago, on July 31 (August 13 according to our Gregorian calendar) of the year 1900. He passed away on the threshold of the 20th century – a century whose vicissitudes and troubles he had foreseen with striking clarity, but also a century, which, tragically, in its historical course and dominant ideologies, would reject his most profound and important teachings. His, therefore, was a teaching at once prophetic and largely unheeded.

A Prophetic Teaching

At the time of the great Russian philosopher, the general view — in keeping with the limitless optimism of the *"belle epoque"*' — foresaw a bright future for humanity in the new century: under the direction and inspiration of the new religion of progress and solidarity stripped of transcendent elements, humanity would enjoy an era of prosperity, peace, justice, security. In the "Excelsior" — a form of dance, which enjoyed an extraordinary success in the last years of the 19th century (and which later lent its name to countless theaters and hotels) — this new religion found its own liturgy, as it were. Victor Hugo proclaimed: "This century was great, the one coming will be happy."

But Soloviev refused to allow himself to be swept up in this desacralized vision. On the contrary, he predicted with prophetic clarity all of the disasters which in fact occurred.

As early as 1882, in his "Second Discourse on Dostoevsky," Soloviev foresaw — and condemned — the sterility and cruelty of the collectivist tyranny which a few years later would oppress Russia and mankind. "The world must not be saved by recourse to force." Soloviev said. "One could imagine men toiling together toward some great end to which they would submit all of their own individual activity; but if this end is imposed on them, if it represents for them something fated and oppressive... then, even if this unity were to embrace all of mankind, universal brotherhood would not be the result, but only a giant anthill." This "anthill" was later constructed through the obtuse and cruel ideology of Lenin and Stalin.

In his final work, The Three Dialogues and the Story of the Antichrist (finished on Easter Sunday 1900), one is struck by how clearly Soloviev foresaw that the 20th century would be "the epoch of great wars, civil strife and revolutions" All this, he said, would prepare the way for the disappearance of "the old structure of separate nations" and "almost everywhere the remains of the ancient monarchical institutions would disappear." This would pave the way for a "United States of Europe."

The accuracy of Soloviev's vision of the great crisis that would strike Christianity at the end of the 20th century is astonishing.

He represents this crisis using the figure of the Antichrist. This fascinating personage will succeed in influencing and persuading almost everyone. It is not difficult to see in this figure of Soloviev the reflection, almost the incarnation, of the confused and ambiguous religiosity of our time.

The Antichrist will be a "convinced spiritualist" Soloviev says, an admirable philanthropist, a committed, active pacifist, a practicing vegetarian, a determined defender of animal rights.

He will also be, among other things, an expert exegete. His knowledge of the bible will even lead the theology faculty of Tübingen to award him an honorary doctorate. Above all, he will be a superb ecumenist, able to engage in dialogue "with words full of sweetness, wisdom and eloquence."

He will not be hostile "in principle" to Christ. Indeed, he will appreciate Christ's teaching. But he will reject the teaching that Christ is unique, and will deny that Christ is risen and alive today.

One sees here described — and condemned — a Christianity of "values," of "openings," of "dialogue," a Christianity where it seems there is little room left for the person of the Son of God crucified for us and risen, little room for the actual event of salvation.

A scenario, I think, that should cause us to reflect...

A scenario in which the faith militant is reduced to humanitarian and generically cultural action, the Gospel message is located in an irenic encounter with all philosophies and all religions and the Church of God is transformed into an organization for social work.

Are we sure Soloviev did not foresee what has actually come to pass? Are we sure it is not precisely this that is the most perilous threat today facing the "holy nation" redeemed by the blood of Christ — the Church?

It is a disturbing question and one we must not avoid.

A Teaching Unheeded

Soloviev understood the 20th century like no one else, but the 20th century did not understand Soloviev.

It isn't that he has not been not recognized and honored. He is often called the greatest Russian philosopher, and few contest this appellation.

Von Balthasar regarded his work "the most universal speculative creation of the modern period" (Gloria III, p. 263) and even goes so far as to set him on the level of Thomas Aquinas.

But there is no doubt that the 20th century, as a whole, gave him no heed. Indeed, the 20th century, at every turn, has gone in the direction opposed to the one he indicated.

The mental attitudes prevalent today, even among many ecclesially active and knowledgeable Christians, are very far indeed from Soloviev's vision of reality.

Among many, here are a few examples:

- Egoistic individualism, which is ever more profoundly leaving its mark on our behaviors and laws;

- Moral subjectivism, which leads people to hold that it is licit and even praiseworthy to assume positions in the legislative and political spheres different from the behavioral norms one personally adheres to;

- Pacifism and non-violence of the Tolstoyan type confused with the Gospel ideals of peace and fraternity to the point of surrendering to tyranny and abandoning the weak and the good to the powerful;

- A theological view which, out of fear of being labeled reactionary, forgets the unity of God's plan, renounces spreading divine truth in all spheres, and abdicates the attempt to live out a coherent Christian life.

In one special way, the 20th century, in its movements and in its social, political and cultural results, strikingly rejected Soloviev's great moral construction. Soloviev held that fundamental ethical principles were rooted in three primordial experiences, naturally present in all men: that is to say, modesty, piety toward others and the religious sentiment.

Yet the 20th century, following an egoistic and unwise sexual revolution, reached levels of permissivism, openly displayed vulgarity and public shamelessness, which seem to have few parallels in history.

Moreover, the 20th century was the most oppressive and bloody of all history, a century without respect for human life and without mercy.

We cannot, certainly, forget the horror of the extermination of the Jews, which can never be execrated sufficiently. But it was not the only extermination. No one remembers the genocide of the Armenians during the First World War.

No one commemorates the tens of millions killed under the Soviet regime.

No one ventures to calculate the number of victims sacrificed uselessly in the various parts of the earth to the communist Utopia.

As for the religious sentiment during the 20th century, in the East for the first time state atheism was both proposed and imposed on a vast portion of humanity, while in the secularized West a hedonistic and libertarian atheism spread until it arrived at the grotesque idea of the "death of God."

In conclusion: Soloviev was undoubtedly a prophet and a teacher, but a teacher who was, in a way, irrelevant. And this, paradoxically, is why he was great and why he is precious for our time.

Born in Milan on June 15, 1928, Biffi was ordained on December 25, 1950. A Milan seminary professor, he became a bishop in 1976, then archbishop of Bologna in 1984 and a cardinal on May 25, 1985. In Bologna, he is the 110th successor of St. Petronius.

Made in the USA
San Bernardino, CA
08 June 2020

72925722R00115